THE BRIDGE BOOK

VOLUME 1 — FOR BEGINNING PLAYERS

by Frank Stewart
and Randall Baron
Drawings by Jude Goodwin

Published by
Devyn Press, Inc.
Louisville, Kentucky

Dedications

To C.H.
—F.S.
To Mary, Devyn and Dustin.
—R.S.B.

Acknowledgments

Grateful thanks to:
Betty Mattison for her patience and typesetting skills;
Pat Houington, Tony Lipka and Henry Francis for their editorial
   assistance;
Izzy Ellis and V.B.I. for their cover photography;
also to Mary Black, Mimi Maier, Bonnie Baron Pollack and
   Debbie Quire.

The reader is referred to as "he" to make the text more
readable.

Printed in the United States of America.

Devyn Press, Inc.
151 Thierman Lane
Louisville, KY 40207

ISBN 0-910791-33-3

Table Of Contents

Preface

We're sure you'll be glad you took the time to learn bridge. This is a truly marvelous game, played by tens of millions, with many potential rewards. Bridge can teach you so many good things — the game has elements of logic, partnership cooperation, discipline, psychology, mathematics and ethics. In fact, you can learn a lot about people from observing how they meet triumph and tragedy at the bridge table. At the least, you'll have an engrossing hobby and a way of making friends wherever you go. And who knows? You may have the makings of a world champion!

No doubt the best way to learn a new skill or improve one's current knowledge is to take private lessons from an authority in the field. If you're eager to become a bridge player and this attractive method appeals, then this book is for you.

Each chapter can be compared to a one-on-one conversation with an expert bridge player and teacher. The presentation is clear and comprehensive and most of your questions have been anticipated. You can proceed at your own pace and review whenever you wish.

The opening section is an orientation for the absolute beginner — no prior knowledge of bridge is assumed.

Throughout, questions are posed in **BOLDFACE** type. You are advised to try answering before going on. In addition, there are quizzes at the end of each chapter so you may test yourself.

We wish you much enjoyment and just as much success. Good luck, and welcome to the world of bridge.

If You're a Complete Beginner . . .

Bridge is played by four people. The usual deck of 52 cards is used. The deck is divided into four suits. SPADES is the HIGHEST-RANKING. It is represented by this symbol: ♠

THE RANKS OF THE SUITS

SPADES . . . . ♠
HEARTS . . . . ♡
DIAMONDS . . . . ◇
CLUBS . . . . ♣

the LOWEST RANKING suit.

Perhaps it is easiest to remember the rank of the suits by noting that they are in reverse alphabetical order.

Because of their rank, spades and hearts are called the "MAJOR" suits, while diamonds and clubs are the "MINOR" suits.

The deck is also divided into 13 RANKS OF CARDS, all the way from the ace, which ranks highest in bridge, down to the two, (also called the "deuce"), which ranks lowest.

THE RANKS OF THE CARDS

A
K
Q
J
10
9
8
7
6
5
4
3
2

When four people get ready for a game of bridge, the first thing they do is CUT FOR PARTNERS. Bridge is a partnership game, and partnership trust and cooperation are among its most important elements. Each player selects a card from a deck that is fanned out face down. The two players who draw the two highest-ranking cards become partners. If two cards of the same rank are drawn, the card of the higher-ranking suit is considered to be higher. The player who draws the highest card of all will be dealer for the first hand.

It is customary to play with two decks, alternating them on each hand. That way one deck can be shuffled while the other is being dealt, and there will always be a fresh deck on hand.

Partners sit opposite each other. The dealer for the first hand distributes all 52 cards, 13 to each player, one at a time, face down. He begins with the player on his left, so the dealer should get the last card himself if he has dealt correctly. Then the players pick up their cards and look at them. Most players sort their cards into suits to make it easier to see what they have.

There are two phases to the game of bridge — the BIDDING (or the AUCTION) and the PLAY OF THE HAND. When playing bridge, the bidding comes first. However, we'll describe the play of the hand first.

Bridge is a member of a large family of card games whose object is to win TRICKS. A trick is composed of one card played by each person in sequence, going clockwise around the table. When you play to a trick, you detach a card from your hand and place it face up toward the center of the table. Since each player has 13 cards, there are 13 tricks to be won.

As you play to each trick, here is an important rule to remember.

YOU MUST PLAY A CARD OF THE SAME SUIT THAT WAS LED TO THE TRICK, IF POSSIBLE. *YOU MUST FOLLOW SUIT.*

Only a card of the same suit that was led to the trick can win that trick. For example, if the card led is the ♣2, the play might proceed:

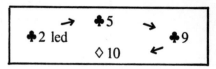

If a player inadvertently fails to follow suit when he has a card of that suit remaining, he is said to revoke, or "renege," and his side is liable to a penalty. But if he is unable to follow suit, he may play any card he chooses. The South player (in all bridge literature, the players are designated by their geographical positions) has done that here, but his ◊ 10 cannot win the trick, even though it ranks higher than any of the other cards. South has failed to follow suit.

There is, however, an important exception to this basic rule of play. One of the suits is usually designed as TRUMPS. Any card in the trump suit outranks even the highest cards in a non-trump suit. Suppose, in our example above, that diamonds were trumps. South, unable to follow suit to the club lead, could play any diamond and win the trick with it. Even the ◊ 2 would be good enough. If two or more trumps are played to the same trick, the highest-ranking trump wins the trick. As you can see, it is clearly to your advantage to have a great many cards in the trump suit, since even your smaller trumps may win tricks.

While there is usually a trump suit in the play, many hands are played without one, that is, at NOTRUMP. The general rule about following suit still applies. If the play is at notrump, you may see a strange situation like this:

```
                      ↗  ◊ J   ↘
        ♣2 led                      ♡ Q
                         ♠ K    ↙
```

Which card would win the trick? Yes, the ♣2, since none of the other hands could follow suit.

Always keep in mind the partnership nature of the game. Any tricks you or your partner take are counted together. Therefore, you should be careful not to spend one of your high cards on a trick that your partner has already won. The player who wins the trick leads to the next trick.

In the play, each partnership tries to win as many tricks as possible, based on the principles we have just seen. To begin the play, one player takes a card from his hand and leads it to the first trick. This is the OPENING LEAD. What happens now is a little strange.

The next player puts his whole hand down on the table face up, arranged in suits, something like this:

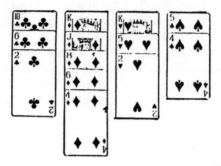

This player, known as the DUMMY, will take no further part in the play of this hand. Instead, his cards will be played by his partner, who is known as the DECLARER.

The play proceeds in this way. Declarer selects a card from his dummy (the term "dummy" is applied to the dummy's hand as well), then the third hand to play contributes a card, declarer plays from his own hand, and the trick is complete. The hand that wins a trick (even if it is dummy) leads to the next trick, and so on, until all 13 tricks have been played to.

Of course, there are some questions left unanswered here. Who becomes declarer? Who is dummy? Which player makes the opening lead? To answer these questions, we must look at the other phase of each hand of bridge, the BIDDING (or AUCTION), which precedes the play.

In the bidding, the players on both sides have a chance to bid for the right to name the trump suit or to play at notrump. Each bid suggests a certain number of tricks that they expect their side to win in the play.

Any bid, therefore, consists of a number and a STRAIN — one of the four suits or notrump. The number is the number of tricks you think your side will take in the play MORE THAN SIX. If you do not think that your side would take even half the tricks, there would be no reason to bid at all. So if you do bid, it is assumed you will take at least six tricks. The tricks you bid for are those beyond that. The *strain* is most often a suit you think will be a good trump suit for your side. Almost invariably, this will be a suit in which you have *length*. If you have a few cards in every suit, but no great length in any single suit, we will see that you may bid notrump.

8

> 3♠ = 9 TRICKS with spades as TRUMPS
> 6♣ = 12 TRICKS with clubs as TRUMPS

A bid of 3♠ says that your side will take at least nine tricks with spades as the trump suit. A 6♣ bid says that you think your side can take at least 12 tricks (all but one), with clubs as trumps.

The bidding works like this: each player get a chance to CALL in turn. The dealer gets first chance, and from there the right to call passes around the table to the left. Each player may bid at his turn. Or, he may say "PASS," indicating that he does not wish to bid at that turn. In a game like Rook, once a player has passed, he may no longer bid on that hand. But in bridge, you may bid whenever it is your turn.

Sometimes all four players pass. When this happens, the hand is thrown in, and another, hopefully more exciting, hand will be dealt. But if someone makes a bid, the AUCTION has begun. From then on, any bid must be higher than the last bid. To make a higher bid, you may bid to take more tricks in any strain. If, for example, someone has bid 3♠, you may bid four or five or six or seven of anything you like. You may also bid to take the same number of tricks in a higher-ranking strain.

Suppose that a bid of 2◊ has been made. You may bid 2♡ or 2♠, but if you want to bid clubs, you would have to bid at least three. Notrump, incidentally, outranks any suit. So you may bid 2 NT even if the last bid is 2♠ (or two of any suit).

It may help to think of a staircase!

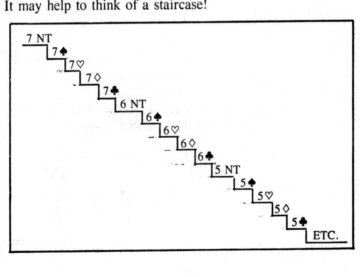

9

Pretend you are climbing the stairs. You can go up, but you cannot go backward.

The bidding may be short and sweet, or it may be long and complicated. One side may find itself with most of the aces, kings, queens, and jacks, and they will have the bidding all to themselves. Sometimes the bidding may be competitive, with both partnerships trying to name the trump suit.

However, when a bid is followed by three consecutive passes, that is the end of the auction. The side that bid higher has won the CONTRACT, and must now take the tricks it contracted for if it is to score any points on the deal. Meanwhile, their opponents become the DEFENDERS, and will try to prevent the declaring side from making its contract. If they do so, they will score points.

THE PLAYER WHO FIRST MENTIONED THE STRAIN WHICH BECOMES THE CONTRACT WILL BE THE DECLARER. HIS PARTNER WILL BE DUMMY. For example, if the auction has gone:

South	West	North	East
1 ♡	Pass	Pass	Pass

South would be declarer. He must try to take seven tricks with hearts as trumps to fulfill his contract. Remember, he plays both his own cards and those in dummy.

If the auction was:

South	West	North	East
1 ♡	Pass	2 ♡	Pass
Pass	Pass		

South would still be declarer. Though North bid 2 ♡, which became the contract, South was the first player to mention hearts.

THE LEAD TO THE FIRST TRICK, THE OPENING LEAD, IS MADE BY THE DEFENDER TO DECLARER'S LEFT.

Suppose we try to follow the play of a typical hand.

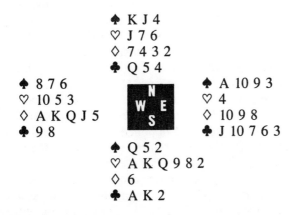

```
                    ♠ K J 4
                    ♡ J 7 6
                    ◊ 7 4 3 2
                    ♣ Q 5 4
    ♠ 8 7 6                         ♠ A 10 9 3
    ♡ 10 5 3          N             ♡ 4
    ◊ A K Q J 5    W     E          ◊ 10 9 8
    ♣ 9 8             S             ♣ J 10 7 6 3
                    ♠ Q 5 2
                    ♡ A K Q 9 8 2
                    ◊ 6
                    ♣ A K 2
```

The bidding has ended, and South has become declarer with hearts as trumps. The opening lead is made by West, the player to declarer's left. He would surely play his ◊A, expecting to take an easy trick.

The dummy is placed down. West's ◊A would win the first trick, as the other hands play the 2, 8 and 6 in order. Having won the first trick, West would undoubtedly lead his ◊K.

If the contract were notrump, declarer would be in bad shape. He can't follow suit to the diamond leads, so he would have to let West win tricks with all his diamonds.

As it is, declarer can start using his trumps. He takes the second trick with his ♡2. A distributional hand like South's often suggests that it would be better to play with his long suit as trumps.

Next, declarer would DRAW THE OPPONENTS' TRUMPS. It would be unwise to let the opponents hold onto the trumps they have and possibly make tricks with them. So declarer plays his ♡A, ♡K and ♡Q, keeping count of the number of trumps the opponents still have. After three "rounds" of trumps, he has drawn them all, so it is safe to lead some other suit.

Declarer can now CASH his high clubs. Next, he can lead a spade and play dummy's ♠K. East can take his ace, but declarer's queen and jack are now the highest-ranking spades still in play, and he can take tricks with them when he regains the lead. Altogether, South would take 11 tricks, losing only to the ◊A and the ♠A. Note that if declarer had failed to draw the opponents' trumps, West would trump when declarer led the third of his high clubs, winning a third trick for the defenders.

Now there are a couple of loose ends to tie up.

First, there are a couple of options in the auction other than passing and bidding. If the opponents get to a contract that you think they will surely fail to make, you may say "DOUBLE" at your turn. You may not double a contract that your partner has bid, only a contract bid by your opponents. If you are correct, and the contract is played doubled and does "go down" or "go set," the points you score are increased. However, if the opponents make their contract they score more points. So you had better be right when you double. In addition, if you double your opponents' contract, either one of them may say "REDOUBLE" in turn, reexpressing their confidence in making what they have bid. If a contract is doubled and redoubled, several times the usual number of points are on the line.

Another very important point: certain contracts are more desirable than others because they carry a bonus. The most common of these are GAME CONTRACTS. There are five game contracts, one for each strain:

GAME CONTRACTS	
3 NT	9 tricks
4 ♡	10 tricks
4 ♠	10 tricks
5 ♣	11 tricks
5 ♢	11 tricks

Bidding and making any contract will score you some points, but a bonus is attached to games bid and made. If, for example, you and your partner bid to 4 ♠, play there and succeed in taking at least ten tricks in the play, you would get a bonus. Note that it is not necessary to take exactly ten tricks, just at least ten.

In addition to game bonuses, there are bonus for bidding and making SLAMS.

SLAM CONTRACTS	
SMALL SLAM	is any contract at the six level. Declarer must take at least 12 tricks to fulfill the contract.
GRAND SLAM	is any contract at the seven level. Declarer must take all 13 tricks to fulfill his contract. As you might imagine, these are quite rare. To bid and make a grand slam is one of the biggest thrills in bridge.

Let's follow the play of another deal.

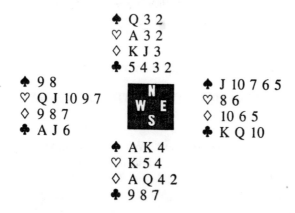

```
              ♠ Q 3 2
              ♡ A 3 2
              ◊ K J 3
              ♣ 5 4 3 2
  ♠ 9 8                        ♠ J 10 7 6 5
  ♡ Q J 10 9 7       N         ♡ 8 6
  ◊ 9 8 7         W     E       ◊ 10 6 5
  ♣ A J 6            S          ♣ K Q 10
              ♠ A K 4
              ♡ K 5 4
              ◊ A Q 4 2
              ♣ 9 8 7
```

Assume that the bidding has ended and South has become declarer in a contract of 3 NT.

The player to declarer's left makes the opening lead, in this case, the ♡Q. You will see the logic of this lead in due time.

The dummy's hand is placed down.

Now South must try to take at least nine tricks at notrump, that is, without any suit being trumps. That means the highest card of the suit led to each trick will win the trick. There are no trumps to worry about.

Perhaps you have realized that the presence of the dummy is something that adds an element of skill to bridge not found in other card games. The skill required in good dummy play is one of the things that makes bridge a unique and challenging game.

This hand is not particularly difficult. In fact, declarer can make his 3 NT contract in the easiest way imaginable, just by taking tricks with high cards that the defenders can't beat.

Let's look at the situation suit by suit.

—In spades, you have three sure tricks with the ace, king and queen.
—In hearts, you have two sure tricks with the ace and king.
—In diamonds, you have four sure tricks, with the ace, king, queen and jack.

There are no tricks in clubs, but we have counted nine tricks in the other suits. That is enough to make the contract.

All that must be done here is to cash winners. Declarer should, however, take care not to spend two of his honors on the same trick

13

— for example, the best way to take the diamond honors is to get the king and jack out of the way, following with the two and four, then take the queen and ace. Note that East and West, if they cannot follow suit when declarer cashes a high card, must DISCARD from some other suit.

This was a game contract, an important contract in the scoring.

TEST YOUR COMPREHENSION OF THE MATERIAL IN THIS SECTION:

1. What is the highest-ranking suit? What suit is next highest-ranking? What strain ranks the highest?
2. The play is at notrump. West leads the ♣2, North, whose hand is dummy, plays the ♢9, East plays the ♡Q, South plays the ♠J. Who wins the trick?
3. Hearts are trumps. West leads the ♠K, North, whose hand is dummy, plays the ♠A, East plays the ♡2, South plays the ♡5. Who wins the trick?
4. How many tricks do each of these bids promise to take? 2♡, 4♣, 7 NT.
5. A bid of 3♢ has been made. Which of the following bids would now be allowed? 3♣, 3♡, 3 NT, 5♣, 2♠, 2 NT?
6. South opened the bidding 1 NT, West passed, North raised to 2 NT, East passed, South bid 3 NT, and everyone passed. Which player is declarer?
7. Which of the following contracts are game contracts? 3♠, 5♣, 4♡, 4 NT?
8. How many tricks are required for a small slam? For a grand slam?

SOLUTIONS:

1. Spades, hearts, notrump.
2. West, since none of the other players could follow suit.
3. South, since he played the highest-ranking trump.
4. 8, 10, 13
5. 3♡, 3 NT, 5♣.
6. South, who bid notrump first.
7. 5♣, 4♡ and 4 NT are game contracts. You need only bid 3 NT to make game, but if you bid some higher number and make your bid, you still score game.
8. 12, 13.

Chapter 1

HAND EVALUATION
OPENING NOTRUMP BIDS AND RESPONSES

Accuracy in the auction is important. You and your partner want to bid to a game or a slam contract if possible and collect your bonus; otherwise you want to stop low and make a PARTSCORE contract.

In this part of the chapter, we'll see how to bid to a contract knowing that your side will have enough aces, kings and trumps to produce the necessary tricks. To produce this accuracy in the bidding, you must know two things:

> THE VALUE OF YOUR HAND
>
> and
>
> THE LANGUAGE OF BIDDING

THE VALUE OF YOUR HAND is the number of tricks your hand rates to produce in the play. We will learn a simple way to estimate the worth of your hand.

THE LANGUAGE OF BIDDING is the way you and your partner tell each other about the valuable features of your hand. Eventually you can decide how high you should bid and which suit (if any) should be trumps.

There are really two meanings in every bid you make. If, for example, you are dealer, and you make an OPENING BID OF 1 NT, you suggest that your side will take seven tricks in the play at notrump. But you also tell your partner something about what kind of hand you hold. In fact, you tell him that you have a definite number of aces, kings and so on, and you suggest that your suits are distributed in a certain way. The bidding in bridge is much more scientific than in other card games.

An important part of learning to play bridge is learning the bidding SYSTEM — the information that each bid gives to your partner about your high-card strength and distribution. If you learn the system, you will be able to reach the right contract on most occasions. The bidding system we will learn is used by the vast majority of bridge players in America.

HAND EVALUATION

Since most tricks are taken with high cards — aces, kings, queens and jacks — the universally-used method of hand evaluation is based on how many of them you hold. A numerical value is assigned to each of the high cards. When you first pick up your hand, you should always use the HIGH-CARD POINT COUNT. The method works like this:

HIGH-CARD POINTS
For each ace . . . . .count 4 points
For each king . . . . .count 3 points
For each queen . . . . .count 2 points
For each jack . . . . .count 1 point

If you hold this hand:

♠ A 7 6
♡ K 6 5
◇ Q 7 6 5
♣ J 7 6

You hold a total of 10 HIGH-CARD POINTS. The full deck contains 40 high-card points, 10 in each suit. Therefore, you have an average hand.

How many high-card points do each of these hands contain?

(a)		(b)		(c)	
♠	K 7 6	♠	A J 6	♠	A 9 8
♡	Q 7 6	♡	Q 6 5	♡	K J 8
◇	J 7 6	◇	K J 7	◇	A Q 7
♣	J 6 5 3	♣	J 7 6 5	♣	K Q 5 4
(7 HCP)		(12 HCP)		(19 HCP)	

Yes, you have 7 points in the first hand, 12 points in the second hand and 19 points in the last hand.

If you have the first hand, it looks as if the opponents have most of the high cards and they will do most of the bidding. Your side may not bid at all unless your partner has been dealt more than his share of the high-card strength.

16

With Hand C, however, you should be encouraged. You have almost half the high cards in the deck. If partner has a little something as well, your side will surely be able to bid and make some high contract, quite possibly a game or even a slam.

PLEASE NOTE THAT OUR POINT-COUNT METHOD HAS NOTHING TO DO WITH SCORING THE GAME. It is merely a device used to translate your high-card strength into an easy-to-work-with numerical value.

Of course, the crucial piece of information that suggests how many tricks your side is likely to make is not just how many high-card points you have, but how many you and your partner hold between you. Here are some important numbers to keep in mind.

```
IMPORTANT NUMBERS TO REMEMBER

26 points.............Game in 3 NT, 4♡ or 4♠
29 points ................Game in 5♣ or 5◇
33 points ........................Small Slam
37 points........................Grand Slam
```

26 POINTS. This is perhaps the most important number of all. If you can discover that you and partner have 26 or more points, your values should produce a game contract in some strain. Really, this is true only of the cheaper game contracts, 3 NT and four of a major suit. To make game in diamonds or clubs, which requires 11 tricks, you need a little extra in high cards — 29 POINTS are usually needed.

With 33 POINTS you should have a chance at 12 tricks, so you should bid to a small slam. And with 37 POINTS your side has almost every high card in the deck. 13 tricks are likely; you should probably bid to a grand slam.

With fewer than 26 points, you will normally settle for a partscore contract.

THE BIDDING SYSTEM: THE LANGUAGE OF BIDDING

Long ago, people noticed that about 26 points in the combined hands would often produce nine or ten tricks in the play. The presence of a trump suit can mean an extra trick or two — that is why the point-count requirement for nine tricks in notrump or ten in a major suit is the same. The next problem is how to discover how many points you and your partner have together, so you can tell if the partnership has at least 26 points. This is what the bidding system is designed for.

Let's look at a simple example.

OPENING NOTRUMP BIDS

Open 1 NT with 16, 17 or 18
HIGH-CARD POINTS   and
Open 2 NT with 22, 23 or 24   BALANCED
HIGH-CARD POINTS   DISTRIBUTION
Open 3 NT with 25, 26 or 27
HIGH-CARD POINTS

To open 3 NT, you must have all the points you need to take nine tricks right in your own hand! As you might imagine, 2 NT and 3 NT openings are relatively rare. But it pays to know how to handle such tremendous hands when they do occur.

Opening 1 NT bids are common. They have a precise meaning. They promise that you hold 16, 17 or 18 high-card points and balanced distribution. By definition, a balanced hand contains no SINGLETON, that is, a suit in which you have only one card; no VOID, that is, a suit in which you have no cards at all; and no more than one DOUBLETON, that is, a suit in which you have two cards.

Which of these hands would be opened with a bid of 1 NT?

(a) ♠ A K 4   (b) ♠ A Q 7   (c) ♠ A J 6 5
    ♡ K 5 4   ♡ K 6 5   ♡ 8 7 6
    ◊ A Q 4 2   ◊ A Q 4 3   ◊ A K 6
    ♣ 9 8 7   ♣ A 6 5   ♣ A Q 5

(d) ♠ K 7 6 4   (e) ♠ Q 6
    ♡ A 6   ♡ A 6 5
    ◊ K 8 6 4 3   ◊ A K 8 7 6
    ♣ A Q   ♣ K J 7

(a) Yes
(b) No, too many points
(c) Yes
(d) No, wrong distribution, with two doubletons
(e) Yes

Note that an opening 1 NT bid does not require a sure trick or even a single high card in every suit. Open 1 NT whenever you have the right kind of hand. You tell your partner a great deal in just one bid.

Now let's move over to your partner's side of the table and see how he can make use of this information. Suppose he has heard you open 1 NT, and his hand is:

♠ Q 3 2
♡ A 3 2
◊ K J 3
♣ 5 4 3 2

How many points does he hold?
He has 10, right? Now, your partner is very well placed. To determine how many high-card points you have as a partnership, he has to do a little mental arithmetic. In this case, he adds his 10 to your 16-18, and arrives at a total of 26-28. So partner knows that a game contract should be bid.

The next question partner will ask himself is, which game looks most attractive? Surely he will be satisfied to stay in notrump. He knows you have a balanced hand, and his is also balanced, so the nine-trick notrump game should be just fine.

So the bidding might go this way:

You	Opponent	Partner	Opponent
1 NT	Pass	3 NT	Pass
Pass	Pass		

Note that, having told your partner what you have with your opening bid, you can pass when he bids game, respecting that he is better able to judge the situation. The opponents, meanwhile, would not bid at all on this hand, since they have relatively few high cards. Remember that you have the option of saying "Double" if they do come in on a whim.

Suppose you and partner have bid to your 3 NT contract, and your combined hands are these:

Partner	You
♠ Q 3 2	♠ A K 4
♡ A 3 2	♡ K 5 4
◊ K J 3	◊ A Q 4 2
♣ 5 4 3 2	♣ 9 8 7

Note that you have exactly 26 points in high cards. Let's see how accurate our point count is in translating points to tricks. You can win three tricks in spades, two in hearts, and four in diamonds, for a total of nine! How about that? It works! Of course, the point count is not always so precisely accurate, but it will often serve you well.

Let's look at one or two other options your partner has when you have opened 1 NT.

Say that partner holds:

♠ Q 3 2
♡ A 3 2
◊ K 4 3
♣ 5 4 3 2

He hears you open 1 NT, and again he adds up the total number of points you hold together. This time it's 25-27. On the last hand, partner knew that the 26-point requirement for game was met for certain even if you had opened a minimum 16-point hand. But this time he is not sure. There could be a game contract available, but only if you have opened 1 NT with a 17 or 18-point hand. Since partner cannot make a final decision, he should pass the buck back to you with a RAISE to 2 NT.

This bid is INVITATIONAL to game. Partner says he thinks there may be a game but he is not quite strong enough to bid it himself. As opener, you will have to look at your hand again and decide what to do. You will go on to 3 NT with 17 or 18 points. With just 16 points, you should pass, sure that you just lack the high cards for a game contract. Notice that if partner has the hand in the diagram you are safe at only an eight-trick contract.

Another hand for partner:

♠ Q 3 2
♡ A 3 2
◇ 5 4 3
♣ 5 4 3 2

This time, he can tell game is impossible. Your side has a maximum of 24 points, so partner would be satisfied with a partscore. Notrump still looks good to him, so he would just pass.

Notice that partner would not raise to 2 NT, even though you might make eight tricks. A raise to 2 NT is invitational to game, and partner is not at all interested in game. You aim should be to bid 3 NT if possible. Otherwise, stay low to maximize your chances of making your contract.

Keeping in mind that a combined total of 33 points is required for a small slam and 37 for a grand slam, let's look at a few slam decisions. Suppose your partner has opened with 1 NT. Here are some hands you might hold.

1.	♠ K 6 5	2.	♠ K 6 5	3.	♠ K 6 5
	♡ A J 6		♡ A J 6		♡ A K Q
	◇ A K 6 5		◇ A Q 6 5		◇ K Q 6 5
	♣ Q 7 5		♣ Q 7 5		♣ A 7 5

With the first hand you know that your partnership has 33-35 high card points, enough to take 12 tricks. So you should bid 6 NT, a small slam. Some players get nervous about bidding to such a high contract, especially in one huge step. Don't be that way. Look on this situation as a great opportunity. Always bid the value of your hand.

How many points do you and your partner have between you when you hold Hand 2?

32-34.

Is there a slam contract available?

There could be, but only if partner has close to 18 points for his opening. What we need here is a bid that invites partner to go on to a small slam, much like a raise to 2 NT invites him to go on to game. To do this, bid 4 NT. Since this bid takes us voluntarily past game, it must imply interest in bigger things. If you knew that no

21

slam contract was possible, you would bid only 3 NT, settling for game. Over your 4 NT bid, partner must look at his hand again and make the final decision of whether to pass 4 NT or bid a slam.

With Hand 3, raise partner to 7 NT! Your side must have at least 37 points.

So far, you have had a balanced hand with which to respond and you have been content to play in notrump. Let's look at some hands with which you might want to suggest or demand that the contract be played in a suit.

1. ♠ K Q 8 7 6 5	2. ♠ J 8 7 6 4 3	3. ♠ K Q 8 7 6
♡ 5	♡ 5	♡ 7 6
◊ A 6 5	◊ J 6 5	◊ A J 6
♣ 7 5 2	♣ 7 5 2	♣ 7 6 5

As we will see in our next chapter, Hand 1 is worth about 13 points, with extra points being added for the good long suit. There are plenty of points for a game contract, but you should prefer to play with your long suit as trumps. If the contract is played in notrump, the opponents might lead hearts and win tricks with their smaller cards because you could not follow suit. But if spades are trumps, you can start using your trumps after the first round of hearts is played.

There is an important point to make here. When you are looking for a good trump suit, it is important to have as many trumps as possible. If the opponents have almost as many or more trumps than your side, you will have trouble making the suit work to your advantage. Remember, your aim in making a suit trumps is to win tricks with your small cards in that suit. So *length* is the primary factor in choosing a trump suit.

> CHOOSING THE TRUMP SUIT
>
> AN ADEQUATE TRUMP SUIT =
> EIGHT OR MORE TRUMPS
> BETWEEN THE TWO HANDS

With Hand 1, you know that your side has at least eight cards in spades (partner will not open 1 NT without at least two, remember), and you know the points for game are available. So, just bid 4 ♠. Partner must pass, trusting your judgment in placing the contract.

Suppose you have a weaker hand, such as Hand 2. A spade contract will play better than notrump. In fact, your hand may not take a single trick at notrump. But if spades are trumps, you will surely take some tricks. Furthermore, with spades as trumps, you are in no danger if the opponents lead hearts.

You cannot bid 4♠ here; the points for game are lacking. But you can and should bid 2♠. Actually, you would like to go back and bid 1♠, but the rules won't let you do it. Partner should pass your 2♠ response.

A RESPONSE OF TWO OF A SUIT TO A 1 NT OPEN-
ING SHOWS WEAKNESS AND NO INTEREST IN
GAME. OPENER SHOULD PASS.

This bid is called a "sign-off" or a "drop-dead" bid. Responder wants to play in his long suit, and at the cheapest possible level.

Hand 3 is worth a game opposite a 1 NT opening bid. **Does your side have eight cards in spades?**

Maybe. Partner can have three or four spades. If so, spades would be a playable trump suit. A trump contract when your side has eight or more trumps will usually produce at least one more trick and is safer than playing in a notrump contract.

But partner could have only two spades. In that case, you would be better off in notrump. The opponents would have almost as many spades as your side.

To find out partner's spade holding, respond 3♠. This bid tells partner you want to bid game, but your suit is not quite long enough to bid 4♠. Partner will look at his spades and raise you to 4♠ if he has three or more. If he opened 1 NT with only two spades, he will bid 3 NT.

A RESPONSE OF THREE OF A SUIT TO A 1 NT
OPENING IS A STRONG BID, ASKING OPENER TO
RAISE WITH THREE OR MORE CARDS.

The purpose of this bid is to get to game or slam in a suit when there is an adequate trump suit, also known as a FIT, available; or to play in notrump otherwise.

Let's review the notrump opening bids and the responses to an opening 1 NT bid. To open 1 NT you must have 16, 17 or 18 high card points and balanced distribution. Balanced distribution is defined as a hand with no singleton or void and no more than one doubleton.

In responding to a 1 NT opening, remember that your partner has described his strength and approximate hand pattern. It is up to you as responder to see that your side arrives in the proper contract. By adding your points to those your partner showed, you can determine at what level you should play.

For example, if you know your side has about 26 points, make sure that a game contract is reached. Also, since you know the opening 1 NT bid shows at least two cards in every suit, you can often tell whether to make one of your suits the trump suit or to play at notrump.

Here are some of your options in responding to 1 NT:

RESPONDING TO 1 NT	
POINTS	BID
0-7	Pass or two of a suit
8-9	2 NT
10-14	3 NT, if balanced, or game in a suit.
15-16	4 NT, if balanced.
17-18	6 NT, if balanced, or six of a suit.
21 or more	7 NT
10 or more	Three of a suit

With 0-7 points, PASS if your hand looks good for play at notrump; but BID TWO OF A SUIT if you have an unbalanced hand with at least five cards in your suit.

With 8-9 points, RAISE TO 2 NT if your hand looks good for play at notrump. This bid is invitational to game.

With 10-14 points, RAISE TO 3 NT if your hand looks good for play at notrump; or JUMP TO GAME IN A SUIT, with a six-card or longer suit.

With 15-16 points, RAISE TO 4 NT if your hand looks good for play at notrump.

With 17-18 points, RAISE TO 6 NT if your hand looks good for play at notrump or BID SIX OF A SUIT with a good six-card or longer suit.

With 21 points or more, RAISE TO 7 NT.

With 10 points or more, BID THREE OF A SUIT with a good five-card or longer suit, planning to play game (or slam) in your suit if partner raises, or to play in notrump otherwise.

TEST YOUR COMPREHENSION OF THE MATERIAL IN THIS CHAPTER:

QUIZ ON BASIC HAND EVALUATION:

1. How many high-card points would an "average" hand contain? How many high-card points are there in the deck?
2. How many high-card points do each of these hands contain?

(a) ♠ A654
    ♥ K65
    ◊ Q65
    ♣ KJ8

(b) ♠ AK65
    ♥ KJ76
    ◊ KQ6
    ♣ AJ

(c) ♠ KJ65
    ♥ Q65
    ◊ QJ8
    ♣ KQ7

(d) ♠ A65
    ♥ J87
    ◊ 876
    ♣ KJ54

(e) ♠ J87
    ♥ J87
    ◊ KQ7
    ♣ AKJ5

3. How many points are required for game in notrump or a major suit?
4. How many points are required for game in a minor suit?
5. How many points are required for a small slam?
6. How many points are required for a grand slam?

SOLUTIONS:

1. 10, 40
2. (a) 13   (b) 21   (c) 14   (d) 9   (e) 15
3. 26   5. 33
4. 29   6. 37

QUIZ ON NOTRUMP OPENING BIDS:

What should be your opening bid if you are dealer, with the first chance to bid, and you hold these hands?

(a) ♠ KJ5
    ♥ AK7
    ◊ KJ65
    ♣ AK7

(b) ♠ AK6
    ♥ A54
    ◊ KJ43
    ♣ Q54

(c) ♠ AJ43
    ♥ AK
    ◊ Q654
    ♣ AKQ

25

(d) ♠ AJ6   (e) ♠ AQ
    ♡ AK54   ♡ KQ5
    ◊ AKQ4   ◊ KQ765
    ♣ KQ   ♣ AQ3

SOLUTIONS:

(a) 2 NT   (c) 2 NT   (e) 2 NT
(b) 1 NT   (d) 3 NT

QUIZ ON OPENING 1 NT:

With which of these hands would you open the bidding 1 NT?

(a) ♠ KQ4   (b) ♠ AQ76   (c) ♠ AJ7
    ♡ AJ7   ♡ AQ87   ♡ 876
    ◊ KQ54   ◊ AK7   ◊ AK54
    ♣ J76   ♣ J7   ♣ KQ7

(d) ♠ AJ7   (e) ♠ 765   (f) ♠ A
    ♡ 876   ♡ A5   ♡ K543
    ◊ A765   ◊ AQ765   ◊ AQ76
    ♣ KQJ   ♣ AQ8   ♣ K765

(g) ♠ J8   (h) ♠ A8   (i) ♠ KQ6
    ♡ A654   ♡ K7654   ♡ 876
    ◊ AKQ7   ◊ A5   ◊ AJ87
    ♣ Q65   ♣ AJ63   ♣ AQ7

SOLUTIONS:

a. Yes
b. No. Too many points.
c. Yes
d. No. Too few points.
e. Yes
f. No. Not with a singleton.
g. Yes
h. No. Not with two doubletons.
i. Yes

QUIZ ON RESPONDING TO 1 NT OPENINGS, PART 1:

Your partner has opened the bidding with 1 NT. On each of these hands, figure the number of high-card points your partnership should have. What should you bid in response to your partner's opening?

(a) ♠ K65
    ♡ A54
    ◊ 654
    ♣ 8765

(b) ♠ AJ76
    ♡ K65
    ◊ 976
    ♣ Q65

(c) ♠ A76
    ♡ K765
    ◊ Q54
    ♣ 987

(d) ♠ AJ7
    ♡ K654
    ◊ A76
    ♣ Q76

(e) ♠ A76
    ♡ AK7
    ◊ KJ65
    ♣ Q65

SOLUTIONS:

a. You have 23-25 points, so game is unlikely. Notrump looks like a suitable spot, so *pass* and play in a partscore at notrump.
b. You have 26-28 points. Bid 3 NT.
c. You have 25-27 points. Game is possible, but only if partner has a maximum 1 NT opening, with closer to 18 points. Raise to 2 NT, a bid that is invitational to game. Partner can look at his hand again and make the final decision. He will bid 3 NT with 17 or 18 points, but will pass with 16.
d. You have 30-32 points. Game is certain, but slam is improbable. Raise to 3 NT.
e. You have 33-35 points! The high cards to make 12 tricks should be available, so bid 6 NT, a small slam.

QUIZ ON RESPONDING TO 1 NT OPENINGS, PART 2:

Partner has opened 1 NT. What would your response be with:

1. ♠ K543	2. ♠ K86432	3. ♠ 1086542
♡ 765	♡ 7	♡ 7
◊ Q54	◊ Q54	◊ 654
♣ 643	♣ 643	♣ 643
4. ♠ K54	5. ♠ J65	6. ♠ K75
♡ QJ2	♡ 54	♡ Q75
◊ K642	◊ 1063	◊ AJ64
♣ 1064	♣ AK653	♣ 1064
7. ♠ KQ4	8. ♠ AQ6	9. ♠ AK2
♡ A5	♡ K75	♡ KJ
◊ AQ53	◊ AQ53	◊ AQ753
♣ Q642	♣ J97	♣ KJ5
10. ♠ AQ9653	11. ♠ J3	12. ♠ KQ1064
♡ 3	♡ Q2	♡ 64
◊ K75	◊ AK8653	◊ AJ2
♣ 1053	♣ 1065	♣ 1054

SOLUTIONS:

1. Pass	6. 3 NT
2. 2♠	7. 6 NT
3. 2♠	8. 4 NT
4. 2 NT	9. 7 NT
5. 2 NT	10. 4♠

11. 3 NT. (You prefer this to the 11-trick game in diamonds.)
12. 3♠ (Partner will raise to 4♠ with three-card support or better, or return to 3 NT with a doubleton.)

Chapter 2

HOW TO TAKE TRICKS
MORE HAND EVALUATION

Suppose you have become declarer. It's up to you to take at least as many tricks as your side has contracted for by using your own cards and those in dummy to best advantage. Let's look at some ways tricks can be won.

> HERE ARE SOME WAYS TO TAKE TRICKS
>
> 1. WITH HIGH CARDS
> 2. WITH INTERMEDIATE CARDS
> 3. WITH A FINESSE
> 4. WITH LONG CARDS
> 5. WITH TRUMPS

1. WITH HIGH CARDS. It is easy to take tricks with aces, kings, etc., that your opponents cannot beat. If you have enough tricks in high cards, the contract will be fulfilled. Sometimes, though, there is a best way to go about cashing your high cards.

HERE ARE 5 WAYS TO PRODUCE TRICKS LIKE MAGIC.

Dummy
♠ K Q J 6

Declarer
♠ A 5

To make sure of four spade tricks, cash the ace first to get it out of the way. Note the problem if you lead your five and win the first trick with one of dummy's honors.

Quite often you will be short of high-card tricks, so you will have to develop additional tricks somehow. One way this may be done is . . .

2. WITH INTERMEDIATE CARDS — cards which aren't high to begin with but that become high as the cards that outrank them are played. For instance, if dummy has the ♠Q1043, and you, declarer, have the ♠KJ75, you have intermediates to ESTABLISH. Lead high cards in this suit until one of the opponents plays his ace. Your remaining intermediates will then be high.

Another way to take tricks with cards that aren't quite high is . . .

3. WITH A FINESSE. Finessing at bridge has nothing to do with being tactful at the table. A finesse is a tactic declarer often tries in an attempt to take a trick with an intermediate card. Look at this example:

Dummy
♡ 6 4

Opponent   *Opponent*
?   ?

Declarer
♡ A Q

Let's say that declarer wants to make two tricks with this holding. **How should he proceed?**

Should declarer lead the ace and follow by leading the queen? Should he lead the queen to begin with? No, neither will work. No matter which opponent has the king, he will be able to use it to capture the queen.

Let's try another strategy. Let declarer lead from dummy (he must find some way for dummy to win a trick in order to do this), and play his queen after his right-hand opponent has already played. **How often would the queen win the trick if declarer tried this?**

The answer is, 50% of the time. One half the time, right-hand opponent will hold the king, and since he will have already played when declarer puts the queen on the trick, the queen will win. The other half of the time, the left-hand opponent will have the king and will be able to capture the queen. But declarer gives himself a 50-50 chance of winning two tricks by taking a finesse with his queen.

A finesse, then, is based on the idea that declarer may win a trick with a card that is not quite high if he plays that card after one opponent has already played. So declarer takes a finesse by leading toward the card he wants to finesse, playing it as third hand.

Here is another example of a finesse:

Dummy
♡ 7 5

Declarer
♡ K 8

To take one trick, declarer must lead toward his ♡K. He hopes that the right-hand opponent holds the ace. If this is the case, the king will be a winner either on this trick or a later one, depending on whether right-hand opponent plays his ace on the first heart lead.

Dummy
♡ 8 7 5

Declarer
♡ K Q 2

To take two tricks, declarer must lead from dummy twice, hoping the ace is held by his right-hand opponent.

Here is a more complicated example of a finessing position:

Dummy
♡ K J 5

Declarer
♡ A 10 4

Declarer would like three tricks with this combination. Two tricks are easy, with high cards. To take a third trick, declarer's best chance is to decide which opponent holds the missing queen and then take a finesse through him. Suppose, for example, that declarer decides that the queen is hiding on his left. He leads the four through his left-hand opponent toward dummy's KJ5. The left-hand opponent will play a low card — it would hardly do him any good to play the queen if he has it. Declarer now finesses dummy's jack. If declarer has guessed correctly about the location of the queen, the jack will win the trick.

Alternatively, declarer may decide to play his right-hand opponent for the queen. In that case, he leads from dummy and plays the ten from his hand, finessing that card. This situation is called a TWO-WAY FINESSE, since declarer can finesse in two directions and must choose between them.

More ways of making tricks:

4. WITH LONG CARDS. Earlier we saw that following suit in the play is a requirement. Declarer can often take advantage of this rule. Suppose the play is at notrump:

Dummy
♡ 7 6

Declarer
♡ A K Q 4 3 2

When he gets the lead, declarer can play his ace, king and queen, forcing the opponents to follow suit. The odds are, by the time declarer has played his high cards, no one else will have any hearts. The low cards will be winners if led since no other player will be able to follow suit.

So your long suits are a potential source of tricks. You will not always have as nice a suit as in the last example, however. Sometimes, you may have to concede a trick or two to the opponents in order to make your long cards good.

Dummy
♡ 6 5 4

Declarer
♡ A K 7 3 2

The contract is still notrump. You cannot hope to take all the tricks in this suit. The opponents are entitled to at least one trick. To establish your long cards, play the ace and king. If both opponents follow suit, concede a trick to the opponents' remaining high card. You lose one trick, but you get back two long-card tricks in return. Of course, you must hope that the opponents' cards in this suit are divided 3-2. If one opponent, unluckily for you, holds the QJ1098, your plan will not work. And if one opponent has four cards in this suit, you must concede two tricks before gaining one.

A final way of making tricks is . . .

5. WITH TRUMPS. A common way of taking extra tricks with your trumps is seen here:

Dummy
♠ —
♡ Q 9 8

Declarer
♠ 7 5
♡ A K J 10 4

Hearts are trumps. Dummy has no spades but still has some trumps. Declarer has some small spades that the opponents can beat. Declarer can turn his losing spades into winners by leading his losers and trumping them in dummy. He saves all the trumps in his hand as winners and makes extra tricks by using dummy's trumps separately.

Suppose we look at a few hands in which declarer can employ each of these techniques in order to make his contract.

1.
♠ A 2
♡ J 7 5 3
♢ 5 4 3
♣ 7 6 5 4

♠ K 6 3
♡ A K Q
♢ A 8 6 2
♣ A K 2

You are declarer in a 3 NT contract. The bottom hand is your hand, the top hand is dummy. The opening lead is the ♠Q. **How would you handle this hand?**

Not many hands are as simple to play as this one, but there is still an important principle to be noted here, one that applies to all hands. BEFORE YOU BEGIN TO PLAY AS DECLARER, PLAN HOW

YOU WILL MAKE YOUR CONTRACT. The usual way to begin your planning is to count your high-card tricks. Then you will know how many extra tricks you must establish, using one of the methods we listed.

Let's count your sure tricks on this hand. Two in spades. Four in hearts. One in diamonds. Two in clubs. That's nine, so this contract should not be difficult to make. All we have to do is cash nine tricks in high cards.

But there is one minor snag.

To take your four heart tricks, you must first get the ace-king-queen out of the way. The jack will then take a trick but dummy must retain some way of winning a trick so the ♡J can be led. Since the only ENTRY to dummy is the ♠A, that card must be saved until after the ace, king and queen of hearts have been played. Therefore, win the first trick with your ♠K, take the high hearts in your hand, and cross to dummy with the ♠A so you can take a trick with the ♡J. You still have three tricks left in hand to fulfill your nine-trick contract.

If you played to the first trick without giving the matter proper thought, you might throw the contract away by winning in the wrong hand and ruining your communication with dummy.

2.
        ♠ A 5 4
        ♡ 5 4 3
        ◊ 5 4
        ♣ Q J 10 9 3

        ♠ K 6 3
        ♡ A K 6 2
        ◊ A 7 6 3
        ♣ K 4

You declare 3 NT again, and the lead is the same, the ♠Q. This time you have only five high card tricks: two spades, two hearts, and one diamond. But four extra tricks are available in clubs, where you have good intermediates. Your plan will be to lead clubs until the ace is played, whereupon dummy's intermediate cards will be established.

Another important principle of play can be seen in this hand. WHEN YOU MUST ESTABLISH SOME WINNERS, BEGIN TO DO SO RIGHT AWAY. IF YOU STOP TO CASH A FEW OF YOUR HIGH CARDS FIRST, YOU MAY ESTABLISH TRICKS FOR THE OPPONENTS!

On this hand, win the first trick with your ♠K. You must save dummy's ace as a way to reach your clubs after they are established. Next, lead the ♣K. If the opponents take their ace, the clubs in dummy are now high. If the opponents do not take the ace right away, keep leading club intermediates until they have to follow suit with the ace. The ♠A that you saved will allow you to reach dummy to take tricks with the rest of the clubs.

Notice that you lead the ♣K first and not a low one. Getting the king out of the way prevents a blockage in your suit.

Now suppose you decide to take tricks with your ◊A, ♡A and ♡K before establishing the club suit. In doing so you establish tricks for the opponents. The ◊KQJ and the ♡QJ are now high and may be cashed against you when the opponents win their ♣A.

3.
       ♠ Q J 4
       ♡ K 5 4 3
       ◊ A K 4
       ♣ K J 5

       ♠ A 10 9 5 3 2
       ♡ 7 6
       ◊ 3 2
       ♣ Q 10 6

This time your contract is 4♠. The opening lead is the ◊Q. You win this trick in dummy. Notice that you have intermediate cards to establish in both spades and clubs. Here, however, playing the TRUMP SUIT should have priority. The reason is that, if you lead clubs while the opponents still have trumps, they may trump one of the winners you establish. On many hands, declarer tries to prevent this by leading trumps until the opponents are all out. On this hand, with your side holding nine trumps to the defenders' four, it would be foolish to leave the opposing trumps where they might pose a threat. So lead the ♠Q from dummy at trick two.

Notice that you have a finesse to take. You hope that your right-hand opponent holds the missing king of trumps, in which case you will lose no tricks in the trump suit. If your right-hand opponent plays low on the lead of the ♠Q, play low from your hand, finessing. If the finesse works, you can repeat it by leading the jack from dummy. If your right-hand opponent ever plays the king, win your ace and you can take the rest of the tricks in the trump suit without difficulty. So long as your right-hand opponent continues to play low, however, continue to finesse. Of course, your left-hand opponent may have been dealt the king and will win a trick with it, but you took your best chance (50%) by finessing.

You plan to draw all the missing trumps as soon as possible. Then you can safely establish your intermediate cards in clubs without fear of an opponent's trumping in. **How should you play the heart suit on this hand?**

You should lead from your hand toward the ♡ K in dummy. What is your objective?

You hope your left-hand opponent holds the missing ace, in which case the king will be worth a trick. This is another example of a finesse.

4 (a).

♠ K 5 4 3
♡ 5 4 3
◇ 4 3
♣ A 10 5 4

♠ A 2
♡ A K Q
◇ A K 6 5 2
♣ 9 6 3

The contract is 3 NT and the opening lead is the ♡ J. Incidentally, **why do you think the opponent has chosen this particular card as his opening lead?**

The techniques that declarer uses to make tricks are also available to the DEFENDERS. Your left-hand opponent here has some good intermediates in hearts, which he hopes to establish. As we will see later on, the lead of the jack tells his partner that he has several intermediate cards in sequence. The jack is his highest.

Back to your problems as declarer. You have eight high-card tricks: two spades, three hearts, two diamonds and one club. One more trick must be established somehow. This time your best chance is to set up a long card. You have five diamonds in your hand and neither opponent is likely to have as many as five since they have only six between them. So if you lead diamonds enough times, you should wind up with the only diamonds left in the play.

After winning the first trick, begin to establish the winner you need immediately. Play the ◇ AK and a low diamond, conceding a trick to the defenders. If the six opposing diamonds are divided evenly, three in each hand, your remaining diamonds will be established right away, and you can cash them when you regain the lead.

It is more likely that the opponents' diamonds will not divide evenly. More often they will divide four in one defender's hand and two in the other. In that case, you will have a little more work to do. Say that one of the defenders wins the third diamond trick, as the other defender DISCARDS, and returns a heart. (The defenders will plug away at the suit they are trying to establish by leading it each time they get a chance.) You win the second heart and concede another diamond to the defenders. Now your fifth diamond is a winner even if one of the opponents started with four diamonds, and you can cash it the next time you gain the lead.

As you can see, setting up a long card can be hard work, but it will often be your best hope to establish a trick that you need.

4 (b).
           ♠ J 5 3
           ♡ A K 2
           ◊ A K 5 4 3
           ♣ 4 3

           ♠ 6 2
           ♡ 5 4 3
           ◊ 6 2
           ♣ A K Q J 10 9

The contract is 5 ♣. The defenders begin by taking the ♠ AK but when they lead the queen, you trump it. Suppose that you continue by drawing the opponents' trumps so they will not be a nuisance to you. Both opponents follow suit twice, so a third round of trumps draws their last one. In drawing trumps it is necessary to keep track of how many trumps remain outstanding. You discard a heart from dummy.

You have ten high-card tricks: six in clubs and two each in hearts and diamonds. The only hope for an 11th trick is to lead diamonds and establish a long card. Now, the fact that clubs are trumps adds a new dimension to the idea of establishing a long suit. If the contract were notrump, you would have to concede tricks to establish your suit, but here you can trump diamonds in your hand and establish the suit without the loss of any tricks.

So you play the ◊ A, the ◊ K and a third diamond which you trump in your hand. If both opponents follow all three times, then the remaining diamonds in dummy are good and you can win a trick in dummy with a high heart to take your established winners. You will discard a little heart, a loser, from your hand. If the opposing diamonds turn out to be 4-2, you must return to dummy with a heart to trump another diamond in hand, finally establishing the fifth one with the other high heart still in dummy as an entry to cash it.

5.

♠ 3
♡ Q 9 8
◊ K 4 3 2
♣ 6 5 4 3 2

♠ A 7 5
♡ A K J 10 7
◊ A 6 5
♣ 8 7

The opening lead against your 4 ♡ contract is the ♠ K. You have only eight high card tricks: five hearts, one spade and two diamonds. But you can get two more by trumping your small spades in dummy. Win the ♠ A at trick one. Dummy is now out of spades, but it still has some trumps. Lead your ♣ 5 and trump with dummy's ♡ 8. Return to your hand with the ◊ A so you can lead the ♠ 7 and trump it in dummy also. Note that on this hand, you must delay drawing the opponents' trumps until you have done the necessary trumping in dummy. You make your original eight tricks, plus two extra tricks with dummy's trumps.

MORE ON HAND EVALUATION

We saw how the HIGH-CARD POINT COUNT is used as a way to evaluate the strength of a hand. The purpose of the POINT COUNT is to translate the trick-taking power of a hand into a numerical value that is easy to work with. But we have just seen that there are ways to take tricks other than with high cards. A long, strong suit may provide you with some extra tricks, and even a short suit may prove valuable if accompanied by length in the trump suit. In the last example hand, you were able to make use of partner's shortness in spades combined with his length in the trump suit. So in order to fully appreciate the value of your hand, you must take into consideration such features. Therefore . . .

LONG SUIT POINTS

WHEN YOU FIRST PICK UP YOUR HAND, ADD AT LEAST ONE POINT FOR EVERY CARD OVER FOUR IN ANY SUIT. The long cards in a very strong suit or in a suit you bid and your partner raises are probably worth even more. Add two points for such holdings, because your chances of turning the long cards into tricks are much improved.

LONG-SUIT POINTS

♠ A 5 4
♡ 9 6 4
◊ A K Q 5
♣ 8 7 6

The above hand is worth 13 points when you first pick it up.

♠ A 5 4 3 2
♡ 9 6
◊ A K Q
♣ 8 7 6

How many points is this hand worth?
The hand is worth 14 points. The fifth card in spades is a potential trick, and one point is added. Suppose you bid 1 ♠, suggesting it as trumps, and partner raises you with a spade bid of his own. As we shall see, such a bid means that he also has some length in spades and agrees with your suggestion that spades might make a good trump suit for your side. Your fifth spade is now very likely to be worth a trick, so the value of your hand, translated into points, would increase a little. You would now count a second point for the fifth spade, giving you a total of 15 points.

♠ A Q 4 2
♡ 9 6 3
◇ A K Q 10 4 3
♣ —

How much do you think this hand is worth? Your chances of making extra diamond tricks are excellent. When you play your high diamonds, you will probably draw all the opponents' diamonds. They will have to follow suit three times, remember. Then your little cards will be winners. For such a solid suit, you may add two points for each card over four. So the hand is worth 19 points.

How about the value of your short suits? Note this well. WHEN YOU FIRST PICK UP YOUR HAND, SHORT SUITS ARE LIABILITIES. The problem is that your partner is all too likely to bid your short suit, maybe more than once. Look at the hand we just discussed. Wouldn't you just know that partner will insist that clubs be trumps? Partners can be like that. Another possible drawback to short suits — if the contract is played in notrump, the defenders will probably lead your short suit. You might have to let them take tricks with their small cards because you cannot follow suit!

Of course, if you are declarer with:

♠ A Q 4 2
♡ 9 6 3
◇ A K Q 10 4 3
♣ —

and diamonds are trumps, your shortness in clubs is not such a bad feature. It will enable you to take some tricks by trumping with your small diamonds, but these are cards with which you expect to make tricks anyway. But suppose your partner bids spades, where you have some excellent help! **Do you see what will happen in the play?**

How will your hand be of help to your partner in a spade contract? Yes, he can use your trumps. Whatever clubs he has can be trumped with your hand as dummy. And he may also be able to use your good diamonds as a source of tricks. So, if your partner bids spades, your shortness in clubs becomes valuable.

SHORT SUIT EVALUATION

COUNT POINTS FOR SHORT SUITS ONLY WHEN YOU HAVE SUPPORT FOR PARTNER'S SUIT AND YOU ARE EVALUATING YOUR HAND AS A DUMMY FOR A CONTRACT IN HIS SUIT.

You cannot really be certain of the value of your short suits until you see what happens in the bidding. But . . .

If partner bids a suit for which you have good support:

A VOID	may be worth as much as 5 points
A SINGLETON	may be worth as much as 3 points
A DOUBLETON	may be worth as much as 1 point

The true value of your short suits depend on just how good your support for your partner's suit is. If you have only three-card support, partner may have trouble taking advantage of your short suits in the play. In our example hand:

♠ A Q 4 2
♡ 9 6 3
◊ A K Q 10 4 3
♣ —

you would add the full five extra points for your club void if partner bids spades. You have excellent support. If he bids hearts, your shortness is probably not worth as much as five points.

♠ K 6 5 4 3
♡ A 5 4
◊ 5
♣ A J 6 4

How much is this hand worth when you first pick it up?
13 points.

Suppose you bid spades and your partner raises. **How much is it worth now?** 14 points.

Say that you bid spades and partner bids clubs. **How much now?** 16 points, with three points added for the singleton diamond.

Suppose you bid spades and your partner bids diamonds. **What is it now worth?** The hand is still worth 13 points. Partner's response has not improved things.

TEST YOUR COMPREHENSION OF THE MATERIAL IN THIS CHAPTER:

QUIZ ON TRICK TAKING:

1. ♠ K Q J 3
    ♡ 9 5 3
    ◊ 7 6 5
    ♣ 8 7 6

    ♠ A 5
    ♡ A K 4
    ◊ A Q 8 2
    ♣ A 5 4 3

    Contract: 3 NT
    Opening lead: ♡Q
    Plan the play.

2. ♠ A 4 3
    ♡ 5 4 3
    ◊ K J 10 9 8
    ♣ 5 4

    ♠ K 7 6
    ♡ A K 8 7
    ◊ Q
    ♣ A 8 7 6 3

    Contract: 3 NT
    Opening lead: ♠J
    Plan the play.

3. ♠ A K Q 4 3
    ♡ K 6 5
    ◊ 5 4
    ♣ 4 3 2

    ♠ 6 5
    ♡ A 4 3
    ◊ A K 6 2
    ♣ A 8 7 6

    Contract: 3 NT
    Opening lead: ♡Q
    Plan the play.

4. ♠ 5 4 3
    ♡ A K 4
    ◊ K J 3
    ♣ 7 6 5 4

    ♠ A K Q 7 6 2
    ♡ Q 6 5
    ◊ Q 10 5
    ♣ 2

    Contract: 4 ♠
    Opening lead: ♣A,
    (followed by the ♣K).
    Plan the play.

5.   ♠ Q 9 2
        ♡ 4 3
        ◊ 5 4 3 2
        ♣ A 7 6 5

        ♠ A K J 10 7
        ♡ A K 6 5 2
        ◊ A 7
        ♣ 8

Contract: 4 ♠
Opening lead: ♣K
Plan the play.

6.   ♠ Q 7
        ♡ 3
        ◊ 6 5 4 3 2
        ♣ A 8 7 6 5

        ♠ A K J 10 9 8
        ♡ A 6 5 4
        ◊ Q 7
        ♣ 2

Contract: 4 ♠
Opening lead: ♣K
Plan the play.

7.   ♠ 5 4
        ♡ A 6 5
        ◊ J 10 4
        ♣ K 6 5 4 3

        ♠ A 2
        ♡ K 7 3
        ◊ A Q 9 5 3
        ♣ A 9 2

Contact: 3 NT
Opening lead: ♠Q
Plan the play.

8.   ♠ K 4 3 2
        ♡ 10 2
        ◊ A Q 3 2
        ♣ A 6 5

        ♠ 8 7
        ♡ A Q J 9 6 5
        ◊ 7 6
        ♣ K 8 3

Contract: 4 ♡
Opening lead: ♣Q
Plan the play.

SOLUTIONS:

1. Declarer has eight high-card tricks and must rely on the dia-mond finesse for his ninth. After winning the first trick, he cashes his spades, being careful to get the ace out of the way first. He then leads a diamond from dummy and plays his queen, hoping the finesse will win.

2. Declarer should establish his diamond *intermediates*. He wins the first trick with the ♠ K, saving the ace as an entry, and leads the ◊ Q, overtaking with dummy's king. Overtaking is essen-tial because, if the opponents duck this trick, declarer is able to continue leading diamonds from dummy and establish the suit.

3. Declarer wins the first trick with the ♡A and plays the ♠A, ♠K, and ♠Q. If the suit splits 3-3, the long cards are good. If one opponent has four spades, declarer must concede a spade trick to establish the fifth card as a trick.

4. Declarer can trump the second high club. Next he should draw the opponents' trumps, keeping count so he will know when they have all been played. With the outstanding trumps no longer a menace, he can set up his diamond intermediates and cash his heart tricks.

5. Declarer plans to *establish his long hearts* by trumping hearts in dummy. He wins the first trick and plays the ♡A and ♡K. Then a low heart is trumped in dummy (with a high trump, just to be safe). If the six missing hearts have all been played, declarer must draw trumps so he can cash his good long cards. He will make 12 tricks. If the hearts divide 4-2, declarer plays a diamond to his ace after trumping the third heart, so he can trump a fourth heart, establishing the fifth one. He then draws trumps as before so that the established card in hearts can be safely cashed. Note that declarer does not draw trumps immediately on this hand. He must wait until dummy's trumps have been used for trumping.

6. Declarer wins the first trick and notes that he has eight high-card tricks. He gets two more by trumping two hearts in dummy. To return to his hand a second time to do this, declarer trumps a club. He then returns to his hand by trumping another club and draws trumps.

7. Declarer wins the first trick and can do no better than stake his contract on the diamond finesse. He goes to dummy and leads the ◊J, playing low from his hand. He hopes the ◊K has been dealt to his right-hand opponent so it can be trapped with repeated finesses.

8. Declarer wins the first trick in dummy and leads the ♡10, planning a finesse against the king. He intends to draw all the trumps as soon as possible and continue with finesses in spades and diamonds.

QUIZ ON HAND EVALUATION:

1. ♠ A J 5 4 3
   ♡ K 6 5 4
   ◊ 5
   ♣ K J 3

What is this hand worth when you pick it up?
If you bid your spades and partner raises?
If you bid spades and partner bids diamonds?
If you bid spades and partner bids hearts?

2. ♠ A K Q J 4 3
   ♡ —
   ◊ A 7 6 5
   ♣ 6 5 4

What is this hand worth when you pick it up?
If you bid spades and partner bids hearts?
If you bid spades and partner bids diamonds?
If you bid spades and partner bids clubs?

3. ♠ 8 6 4 3 2
   ♡ K 6 4
   ◊ A 4 2
   ♣ Q 3

What is this hand worth when you pick it up?
If partner bids hearts?
If partner bids clubs?

SOLUTIONS:

1. 13: 14: 13: 16
2. 18: 18: as much as 23; more than 18, but probably not as much as 23, since your support for partner is not as good as when he bids diamonds.
3. 10 (Note, however, that the fifth spade is unlikely to be a trick since your suit is so poor): 10 (If partner is going to need to use your shortness in clubs, then the ♣Q will probably be of no use to him.): 10.

45

Chapter 3

OPENING THE BIDDING WITH ONE OF A SUIT

We have discussed opening notrump bids and some of partner's options as "responder." A 1 NT opening accurately describes your high-card strength and distribution, so you should be anxious to make this bid when you have the right type of hand.

Obviously, there will be many other times when you may sense that your hand will take a lot of tricks and you should feel, rightly, like opening the bidding. However, you may not have the right kind of hand for an opening bid in notrump; perhaps too many or too few high-card points, or the wrong sort of distribution. You may open many of these hands with a bid of ONE OF A SUIT.

There are 40 high-card points in the deck. When you hold better than an average 10-point hand, your partnership probably has more than its share of the high-card strength and will make more tricks than the opponents. The line of demarcation for opening the bidding is the 13-point level. Of course, it is not entirely safe to make a bid even with a 13-point hand. The opponents, in theory, could have the other 27 high-card points, and you would find a seven-trick contract far too hard to manage.

But by the same token, it is far too conservative to wait until you have a hand worth 20 points or more to open. 13-point hands are a good place to start opening the bidding — if you and your partner were *both* timid about opening such hands, you would sometimes never bid when you had between you the 26 points needed for game!

OPEN THE BIDDING WITH 13 HIGH-CARD POINTS.

YOU SHOULD BE WILLING TO MAKE THE FIRST BID IN THE AUCTION ("OPEN THE BIDDING") WITH 13 HIGH-CARD POINTS. HANDS WITH 14 HIGH-CARD POINTS ARE OBLIGATORY OPENING BIDS. YOU MAY OPEN HANDS THAT ARE ONLY SLIGHTLY BETTER THAN AVERAGE (10-12 HIGH-CARD POINTS) IF THEY HAVE AN ESPECIALLY GOOD SUIT OR SUITS.

In deciding whether to open hands on the 13-point fence or just below, there is one other important factor to consider — *Quick-Trick Structure.*

So far in our discussion of hand evaluation, we have seen that the trick-taking value of a hand is expressed in points counted for high cards and distribution. Quick Tricks are a measure of the *defensive* values of your hand. Remember that after the auction begins, the opponents may bid. You have less reason to get the auction started if your hand suggests that the opponents will be successful if they buy the contract. So any opening bid implies some cards that will take tricks *no matter what the contract turns out to be.* Aces and kings are your best shot for sure tricks, so . . .

Our Table of Quick Tricks looks like this:

AK in same suit 2	Quick Tricks
AQ in same suit 1½	Quick Tricks
A 1	Quick Trick
KQ in same suit 1	Quick Trick
K . . . . ½	Quick Trick

In arriving at a value for your hand, add up your Quick Tricks as well as your high-card and distributional points.

DO NOT OPEN ANY HAND THAT IS SUB-MINIMUM IN HIGH CARDS AND THAT CONTAINS FEWER THAN TWO QUICK TRICKS.

Let's look at a few hands and try to decide whether they are worth an opening bid:

1. ♠ K x
   ♡ K J x x
   ◊ Q J x x
   ♣ Q J x

   This is one of the few 13-point hands that should *not* be opened. Note the terrible lack of Quick Tricks. This hand is not as good as it might seem.

2. ♠ A x x x
   ♡ J x
   ◊ K J x x
   ♣ K x x

   This time you have two Quick Tricks, but you are lacking good suits to help you make some tricks. Pass with this borderline hand.

3. ♠ x x x   This hand, even though it contains fewer
   ♡ A x x   high-card points than either of the first two
   ◊ A K x x x x   hands, is worth opening. You have a good
   ♣ x   suit and your Quick Trick structure is
                     excellent.

4. ♠ A Q x x x   Most players would open this one. You
   ♡ A J x x x   are a little light in high cards, but you have
   ◊ x x   two possible trick-producing suits plus 2½
   ♣ x   Quick Tricks. Another consideration here
                     is that you have the *major* suits. If the
opponents start bidding, you may be able to outbid them a little more
easily since your suits rank higher than theirs.

5. ♠ A J 10 x x x x   This is a little extreme, but the hand is
   ♡ A x x x   worth opening. You have some tricks, a
   ◊ x x   good suit, and you have your required two
   ♣ —   Quick Tricks.

Once you have judged that your hand is worth an opening bid, the next problem is to choose which suit to open. Here are some simple guidelines. Think of them as a list of priorities. If your hand fits into the first guideline, make that bid. If not, go to number two. If your hand fits that description, make that bid. If not, go to guideline three and so on until you make a match.

GUIDELINES FOR WHICH SUIT TO OPEN

1. WITH ONE FIVE-CARD OR LONGER SUIT — open one of that suit.
2. WITH TWO FIVE-CARD SUITS — open one of the higher ranking suit. *EXCEPTION* — with five clubs and five spades, open 1♣.
3. WITH ONE FOUR-CARD MINOR — open one of that minor.
4. WITH TWO FOUR-CARD MINORS — open 1♣.
5. WITH THREE CLUBS — open 1♣.
6. WITH FOUR SPADES, FOUR HEARTS, THREE DIAMONDS and TWO CLUBS — open 1◊.

The auction is like a conversation in which you and your partner exchange information. You will always have to decide how high you should bid and you will also try to locate the best suit to make trump. (There will, of course, be times when you will decide to play at notrump, no suit being attractive; but there are benefits to finding a trump suit.)

You may wonder why you should bid a three-card club or diamond suit instead of a four-card heart or spade suit. The answer is because an opening bid in a major suit PROMISES AT LEAST FIVE CARDS. (Not everyone bids this way, but we recommend "five-card major openings." For the purposes of this book, a major suit opening requires five cards.)

Now let's look at a few hands and choose an opening bid for each.

6. ♠ x x
   ♡ A K
   ◊ K J x
   ♣ Q J x x x x

1♣. No problem here. Guideline 1.

7. ♠ x x x
   ♡ A K x
   ◊ K J x
   ♣ Q J x x

1♣, your longest suit, such as it is. When we search for a playable trump suit, or "fit," we prefer a combined total of *at least eight cards.*Your eight trumps may be divided four in your hand and four in your partner's hand. As we will see in our next lesson, partner will not raise clubs unless he also has length in that suit. Guideline 3.

8. ♠ x
   ♡ Q x x x x
   ◊ K x x x
   ♣ A K Q

1♡. *Length,* remember, is the most important factor in looking for a trump suit. Guideline 1.

9. ♠ K x x x
   ♡ A x x
   ◊ A x
   ♣ Q J x x

1♣. No five-card suit, so open in your only four-card minor. Guideline 3.

10. ♠ A x
    ♡ K J x x
    ◊ A J x x
    ♣ x x x

1◊. Guideline 3.

11. ♠ A J x x   1♣. Guideline 3.
     ♡ K x x x
     ◊ x
     ♣ A Q x x

12. ♠ K Q x   1♣. With two four-card minors, open
     ♡ x x   1♣. Guideline 4.
     ◊ A x x x
     ♣ K Q x x

13. ♠ A x x x x   1♠. With two *long* suits (five or more
     ♡ A K x x x   cards in each one), open in the *higher-*
     ◊ Q x   *ranking.* Guideline 2.
     ♣ x

14. ♠ Q x   1 NT. Despite your nice diamond suit,
     ♡ K J x   this is a balanced hand that you can de-
     ◊ A K J x x   scribe with an opening bid in notrump.
     ♣ Q x x

15. ♠ A x x   1♣. No five-card suit, no four card
     ♡ J x x x   minor, but you have three clubs. Note
     ◊ Q x x   well, though, that we open 1♣ on this
     ♣ A K x   hand because there is no alternative, not
                   because we want to open in a three-card
                   minor. Guideline 5.

16. ♠ K x x x   1◊. No five-card suit, no four-card
     ♡ A J x x   minor, only two clubs, so we must open
     ◊ A J x   1◊. Guideline 6.
     ♣ x x

    The opening bid is the first step in your campaign to discover a
sound contract. *Always open the bidding when you have the required
values.* The side that makes the first bid generally has an advantage
in exchanging information easily and arriving at a good contract.

INTRODUCTION TO DEFENSIVE PLAY:
LEADING TO A TRICK

The DEFENDERS oppose declarer and try to keep him from making his contract. You will be declarer on about one-quarter of the hands you play, and on another quarter, you will be able to relax as dummy. But fully one-half of the time, you will be on defense.

The rules of the game impose a built-in handicap on the defending side. If you are declarer, you can look at dummy and see what assets you have to work with. Often it will be obvious where the bulk of your tricks are coming from and what suits you should work on.

But you can't see what your partner has when you are on defense. Consequently, it can be hard for you to tell which suit offers your side the best hope of some tricks.

> TO ELIMINATE SOME OF THE GUESSWORK, DEFENDERS USE CONVENTIONALLY ACCEPTED PRACTICES AS THEY ROUTINELY PLAY TO EACH TRICK.

For instance IF YOU ARE TO *LEAD* TO A TRICK AS A DEFENDER, and you have selected a suit, THE CARD YOU CHOOSE IS USUALLY PREDETERMINED. The defense will be easier if you tell your partner something about what you have in the suit.

Suppose you have decided on a heart lead at some point (the business of picking out which suit you should lead often requires good judgment and will be discussed later; for now, we will learn about what card to lead from a chosen suit). Your hearts are:

K Q J 7 5

The proper card to lead here is the king. There is a two-fold advantage. By leading one of your higher cards, you force declarer to spend the ace in order to win the trick and your other intermediates are high. True, any of your high cards would do the job, but the king tells partner that YOU HAVE A SEQUENCE OF CARDS OF WHICH THE KING IS THE HIGHEST. Partner might like to know that you have such a promising holding!

Look at this hand:

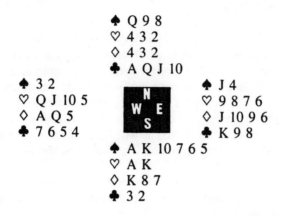

```
                    ♠ Q 9 8
                    ♡ 4 3 2
                    ◇ 4 3 2
                    ♣ A Q J 10
     ♠ 3 2                          ♠ J 4
     ♡ Q J 10 5        N            ♡ 9 8 7 6
     ◇ A Q 5        W     E         ◇ J 10 9 6
     ♣ 7 6 5 4         S            ♣ K 9 8
                    ♠ A K 10 7 6 5
                    ♡ A K
                    ◇ K 8 7
                    ♣ 3 2
```

South is declarer in 4♠. West chooses hearts and leads the queen, the top card in his sequence. (You can see that sequential holdings make excellent leads; they are *safe,* and you may begin to establish a trick or two by leading from them.) Declarer wins the first trick with the ♡A, plays ♠Q and ♠A to exhaust the defenders of their trumps, and leads a club, trying to establish dummy's suit with a finesse. East wins his ♣K. What should he lead? Not hearts. When West led the ♡Q, he denied holding the king. So East knows there are no tricks for the defenders in hearts. He switches to diamonds, leading the jack to suggest a sequence of cards headed by the jack. Declarer covers with the king and West wins the ace and queen and leads a third round, knowing that his partner has the ten and it might be worth a trick. The defenders wind up with four tricks, defeating the contract by one trick.

A *SEQUENCE* consists of three or more cards that are adjacent in rank, the highest one of which is an honor.

Lead the king from KQJx.
Lead the queen from QJ10xx.
Lead the jack from J109xx or KJ109x.
Lead the ten from 1098x or K1098x.

Holdings like these:

KQ10x
QJ9x
J108x

that contain *two* honors in sequence *plus* a third card that almost completes the series are treated like true sequences, and the top card is still led. This is called a "broken sequence." Another type of sequence, called an interior sequence, contains three honors in a suit of which the lower two honors are adjacent to each other but not to the highest honor. Examples of interior sequences include AJ10x, K109x and AQJ10. When leading from an interior sequence, lead the top of the adjacent honors. Therefore lead the jack from the AJ10x.

When the suit you have chosen to lead is headed by only two "equals," with not a sign of another good card, or when your suit is completely full of holes, lead one of your LOW cards against a notrump contract, but consider leading the top of your two honors against a suit contract. Specifically, it is customary to lead your *FOURTH-HIGHEST CARD* when you don't have a sequence.

Lead the five from K10852
Lead the two from J932
Lead the six from QJ764
Lead the six from KQ764 against a notrump contract, but lead the king against a suit contract.

*OPENING LEADS ARE NOT AN EXACT SCIENCE,
BUT THERE ARE RULES TO FOLLOW.*

The reason for leading your fourth-highest card from a broken suit is still to give your partner helpful information. For instance, suppose you are defending a notrump contract, and your partner leads a deuce. You know he has four cards in the suit (if the deuce is his fourth-highest card, he has a four-card suit). This may help you decide whether your partner's suit offers enough potential tricks to set the contract or whether you should consider switching to some other suit if you gain the lead.

Sometimes, knowing that partner has led his fourth-highest card allows you to work out exactly what he has! Look at this situation:

Dummy
♠ K 5 3

You

♠ 7 led   ♠ A J 9 2

You are defending a notrump contract and your partner has led the ♠ 7, which you may assume is his fourth-highest card in the suit. Dummy plays low. **What would you play?**

Playing the ace looks wrong, since declarer would be able to take a trick with dummy's king later. Could we do better? If partner's seven is his fourth-highest spade, **what must his holding be?** He must have Q1087. He has three spades higher than the seven, and the queen, ten and eight are the only three that you can't see in your own hand or in dummy. So you can play your *deuce!* And partner's seven will be good enough to win the trick. He can then lead through dummy's king again.

Here's a problem in defense:

♠ Q 9 8
♡ 10 6 5
◇ 10 6
♣ A Q J 10 7

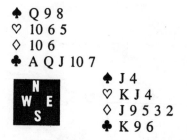

♠ J 4
♡ K J 4
◇ J 9 5 3 2
♣ K 9 6

Declarer is playing a 4♠ contract. Your partner's opening lead is the ♡3. Dummy plays the five, you put up your king (as we will see later on, the purpose of your play is to make declarer pay a steep price if he wants to win the trick), and declarer takes the ace. He exhausts you of your trumps by playing the ace and king from his hand, and then he leads a club, finessing dummy's queen. You win your king. **What should you lead now?**

It is best to play back a heart, hoping that your partner had something good in the suit. Suppose you try your ♡J, and it wins the trick. Your partner follows with the ♡2. **How many hearts do you think he had?** He should have had five, shouldn't he? He led the *three*, his fourth-highest, and he had one card, the deuce, that was lower ranking. So, declarer is now out of hearts, and will be able to trump any further heart leads.

Knowing the heart suit offers no more tricks, you *switch to diamonds*, hoping partner has some high cards in that suit that will be worth tricks.

What card should you lead from this suit?

K 9 8 7 4

The seven is the proper lead. This suit does *not* contain a sequence, which, by our definition, must be headed by an honor.

What about leading from AK863 or A9752? There is a special consideration here — what contract you are defending. If the opponents have arrived in *notrump,* you would select your fourth-highest card from these holdings. It is true you may give away one trick by letting the opponents score some lower honor easily. However, your main objective in defense at notrump is to establish some long cards. You should be willing to concede one trick in your suit to improve your chances of making tricks with all your long cards. The problem with cashing your high cards first is that you may ruin your communication with your partner. You may exhaust him of cards in your suit and make it impossible for him to return your lead.

Against a *suit* contract, however, it is too dangerous to lead away from your top cards. The problem is that, if some other suit is trumps, declarer might be able to trump the second time your suit is led. You might never get your ace unless you take it right away. *Singletons* in declarer's hand or dummy are all too common. Look at this layout, in which spades are trumps.

```
                ♡ K
  ♡ A 9 7 6 2          ♡ Q 10 5 3
                ♡ J 8 4
```

If you lead your fourth-highest card here, you may never get your ace. You also present declarer with an undeserved trick with dummy's king.

```
DO NOT UNDERLEAD ACES AGAINST
         SUIT CONTRACTS.
```

Suppose you decide to lead a suit in which you do not have length. There are a couple of rules to remember.

```
LEAD THE TOP CARD OF ANY DOUBLETON.
```

Lead the queen from Q5
Lead the nine from 92

Following this rule frequently offers an advantage, as the following example shows.

```
              ♡ 10 5 4
   ♡ Q 7                    ♡ K J 6 3 2
              ♡ A 9 8
```

Perhaps partner has bid hearts, so you decide to lead one. Lead the queen and *get it out of the way.* Partner can retain both of his high honors and can cash them easily if your side can regain the lead at some point. If you were to lead your seven, you could still establish some tricks for your side, but your winners would be in different hands. It would not be as easy for your side to take your tricks. If you have three cards in the suit you choose to lead, however, you may lead low.

Lead the three from Q83.
Lead the two from A72 against notrump, but lead the ace against a suit contract.

Look at this situation:

```
              ♡ 7 6
   ♡ Q 8 3                  ♡ A 10 9 5 2
              ♡ K J 4
```

If you were to lead the queen in this layout, you would cost your side a trick.

TEST YOUR COMPREHENSION OF THE MATERIAL
IN THIS CHAPTER:

QUIZ ON OPENING THE BIDDING
WITH ONE OF A SUIT:

I. How many Quick Tricks do the following hands contain?

1. ♠ Axxx   2. ♠ xxx   3. ♠ AQ
   ♥ KQxx   ♥ Kxxx   ♥ AQxxx
   ◊ Kxx   ◊ QJx   ◊ Kxx
   ♣ Kx   ♣ Axx   ♣ Jxx

4, ♠ AKxx   5. ♠ AQxxx
   ♥ Kx   ♥ Ax
   ◊ Qx   ◊ xx
   ♣ KQxxx   ♣ AKxx

II. Which of the following hands would you judge to be worth an opening bid?

1. ♠ Qx   2. ♠ A109xx   3. ♠ AKJxxx
   ♥ QJx   ♥ AQxxx   ♥ Kxx
   ◊ QJxx   ◊ Qx   ◊ xx
   ♣ KQxx   ♣ x   ♣ Jx

4. ♠ x   5. ♠ Qxx
   ♥ AQJ   ♥ AJ10xxx
   ◊ Kxxx   ◊ Axxx
   ♣ Qxxxx   ♣ —

III. Choose an opening bid with each of the following hands:

1. ♠ xx   2. ♠ Qxxxx   ♠ AKx
   ♥ AKxxx   ♥ AKJx   ♥ Kxx
   ◊ Axx   ◊ Ax   ◊ Kxx
   ♣ Qxx   ♣ xx   ♣ Jxxx

4. ♠ AKJx   5. ♠ xx   6. ♠ Axxx
   ♥ Ax   ♥ AQxx   ♥ KJx
   ◊ xxx   ◊ KQxx   ◊ xxx
   ♣ Qxxx   ♣ Kxx   ♣ AJx

7. ♠ AKx
   ♡ xx
   ◇ AJxx
   ♣ Qxxx

8. ♠ x
   ♡ Kxxxx
   ◇ AKxxx
   ♣ Kx

9. ♠ AQJxx
   ♡ AQJxx
   ◇ xx
   ♣ x

10. ♠ Ax
    ♡ Kxx
    ◇ KQxxx
    ♣ A10x

11. ♠ xx
    ♡ Kxx
    ◇ AKxx
    ♣ KJxx

12. ♠ AKx
    ♡ 10xxx
    ◇ Jxx
    ♣ AQx

13. ♠ Axxx
    ♡ Axxx
    ◇ xx
    ♣ AJx

14. ♠ AKx
    ♡ 10xxx
    ◇ Kxx
    ♣ AQx

15. ♠ Kxx
    ♡ Jxxx
    ◇ AQx
    ♣ KJx

16. ♠ AQxx
    ♡ Qx
    ◇ AKxx
    ♣ KJx

17. ♠ xx
    ♡ Axxxx
    ◇ KQJx
    ♣ Ax

18. ♠ Axxx
    ♡ AJxx
    ◇ KQx
    ♣ Jx

SOLUTIONS:

I. 1. 3
    2. 1½
    3. 3½
    4. 3½
    5. 4½

II. 1. Pass. Too few Quick Tricks to open this borderline hand.
    2. Open. Two reasonable long suits and 2½ Quick Tricks.
    3. Open. A good long suit and 2½ Quick Tricks.
    4. Pass. Very close decision. The deciding factor is that you lack length in spades, the ranking suit, and the opponents might be able to outbid you. Also, your suits are of poor quality.
    5. Open. A good long suit, plus two Quick Tricks.

III.
1. 1♡
2. 1♠, your *longest* suit.
3. 1♣, your *longest* suit, such as it is.
4. 1♣, no five-card suit, your only four-card minor.
5. 1◊.
6. 1♣.
7. 1♣. With two four-card minors, open 1♣.
8. 1♡. Open the *higher-ranking* of your two long suits.
9. 1♠
10. 1 NT
11. 1♣.
12. 1♣. No five-card suit or four-card minor, but three clubs.
13. 1♣
14. 1 NT
15. 1♣.
16. 1◊. This is a very good hand, but you must open with just one in case partner holds very little strength.
17. 1♡
18. 1◊ With four spades, four hearts, three diamonds and two clubs, open 1◊.

QUIZ ON LEADING TO A TRICK:

I. The opponents have arrived in a contract of 4♠. You have chosen to lead a heart. Choose the proper card to lead from each of these holdings.

1. ♡ Q J 10 4	15. ♡ Q J 4	
2. ♡ Q J 9 4	16. ♡ A 9 7 5 2	
3. ♡ Q J 7 3 2	17. ♡ A K Q 6	
4. ♡ Q 7 3 2	18. ♡ J 10 5 4 2	
5. ♡ Q 10 8 4 3	19. ♡ K 9 8 7	
6. ♡ J 10 9 5 3	20. ♡ Q 5	
7. ♡ J 10 8 7 4	21. ♡ A 8	
8. ♡ J 9 8 7 4	22. ♡ 10 5	
9. ♡ K Q J 10 4	23. ♡ J 9	
10. ♡ K Q 10 4	24. ♡ K 9 6 4 2	
11. ♡ K J 3 2	25. ♡ 10 9 8 5 3	
12. ♡ Q 8 4	26. ♡ K J 10 9 4	
13. ♡ J 9 2	27. ♡ A Q J 10 5	
14. ♡ A 7 5		

II. The opponents have bid 3 NT. You have chosen to lead a spade. Choose the proper card to lead from each of these holdings, which contain potential long card tricks:

1.	♠ Q J 10 4	11.	♠ A K 9 6 2
2.	♠ K J 9 6 3	12.	♠ K 10 9 8 4
3.	♠ A J 6 3	13.	♠ Q 10 9 7 5
4.	♠ J 10 9 5 3	14.	♠ A J 10 9 4
5.	♠ K Q 5 2	15.	♠ A Q J 10 5
6.	♠ J 9 8 7 3	16.	♠ K Q 10 5 4
7.	♠ Q J 6	17.	♠ Q J 4 3 2
8.	♠ Q 9 8 7	18.	♠ K 9 8 2
9.	♠ Q 6	19.	♠ Q 8 4
10.	♠ A K Q 8 6		

III.
1. Partner has led the ♠2 against the opponents' 3 NT contract. How many spades is he likely to have? Why might it be important for you to know this?
2. Partner has led the ♡K against the opponents' 4♠ contract. Your side did not bid. What is partner likely to have in hearts?
3. Partner has led the ♠4 against the opponents' 3 NT contract. Dummy holds K83 in spades, you have Q92. How many spades is partner likely to have?
4. Partner has led the ♠6 against the opponents' 3 NT contract. Dummy holds K73 in spades, you have AJ92. What is partner's spade holding likely to be?
5. Partner has led the ♡Q against the opponents' 4♠ contract. Your heart holding is KJ964. How many hearts is partner likely to have?

SOLUTIONS:

I.

1.	Q	8.	7	15.	Q	22.	10
2.	Q	9.	K	16.	A	23.	J
3.	Q or 3	10.	K	17.	A	24.	4
4.	2	11.	2	18.	J or 4	25.	10
5.	4	12.	4	19.	7	26.	J
6.	J	13.	2	20.	Q	27.	A
7.	J	14.	A	21.	A		

II.

1. Q
2. 6
3. 3
4. J
5. 2
6. 7
7. Q (to get out of partner's way if he has length).
8. 7
9. Q (this would be an unusual suit to lead against a notrump contract).
10. A (hoping to take all the tricks).
11. 6 (laying down the ace and king might work well though).
12. 10 (top of an interior sequence).
13. 10 (top of a broken interior sequence).
14. J
15. Q
16. K
17. 3
18. 2
19. 4

III.

1. Four; you might want to know how many tricks might become available to your side in this suit.
2. The queen, and probably the jack (or ten) as well.
3. Four
4. Q1086
5. One or two, but no more than two. He would lead low from Qxx or Qxxx.

Chapter 4

RESPONDING TO THE OPENING BID

Now let's move over to the other side of the table and discuss RESPONDING TO THE OPENING BID.

The first thing to keep in mind in RESPONDING is that it is right to keep the conversation going even if your hand is fairly weak. There are two reasons for this. First, partner's opening bid may be based on a very strong hand. He might open with a bid of only one even if he held 20 high-card points or more. If you had nothing at all, he would need all that strength to make his one level contract. So game is still possible even if your hand is poor. The place we draw the line in responding is about 6 points. With as much as 6, you should respond to partner's opening in some way. With less, you may pass.

Another reason for RESPONDING with weakness is that the first suit partner suggests as trumps may not be the best one available. If you have enough strength to respond, one of your options is to bid a suit in which you have length to suggest that suit as trumps. You are especially interested in finding a major suit for trumps whenever possible.

While you may be obliged to bid with weakness, you may also choose to respond with a minimum bid even if your hand is fairly strong and you expect to reach game eventually. The reason: to save space so you and partner can exchange the maximum amount of information before deciding where to play.

Several options are available in RESPONDING, and they fall into three categories. Since finding a major suit fit is so important, you want to (1) RAISE partner's major suit if you can. If partner opened in a minor or if you don't have support for his major, you may (2) SUGGEST ANOTHER SUIT as a possible trump suit. Finally, you choose to (3) BID NOTRUMP. Each bid has a meaning, and we will examine each in turn.

Suppose your partner has opened the bidding 1 ♡, the next player has passed, and it is up to you to respond.

1. ♠ x x   Pass. Your chances for game do not
   ♡ Q x x   justify a response. If you bid with this,
   ◊ J x x x   your partner may get excited and get you
   ♣ x x x x   too high.

2. ♠ x x   Bid 2♡. A single raise of partner's suit
   ♡ Q x x x   shows 6-9 points and support for his suit
   ◊ A x x x x   "Support" is usually four or more cards
   ♣ x x   (since you want to be sure your partnership has at least eight trumps between you
before you choose that suit to be trumps.) However, you may raise
a major-suit opening to two with only three-card support, since partner
has promised a five-card suit.

3. ♠ x x x   A 2♡ response is best.
   ♡ Q x x
   ◊ A x x
   ♣ x x x x

4. ♠ x x x   Bid 3♡. A double raise shows 13-15
   ♡ K J x x   points and good support for partner. Four-
   ◊ A J x x   card support is required to give a double
   ♣ A x   raise in any suit, even a major. This bid
                   in our system is "forcing." Partner can-
                   not pass. He must bid some more. It is
logical that a double raise should be forcing, since opening bidder
knows after a double raise there are sufficient values for game.

5. ♠ —   It might occur to you to wonder why, on
   ♡ Q J x x x   hand #4, you don't just respond 4♡,
   ◊ Q J x x x   which is what you figure to make. The
   ♣ x x x   reason is that a direct leap to game in part-
                   ner's suit shows a hand like #5 instead!
The bid is made when you hold excellent support for partner's suit,
a distributional hand, but fewer than 10 high-card points.

6. ♠ Q x x x   Respond 1♠. You are barely worth a bid
   ♡ x   and it is best to show the suit you can bid
   ◊ A x x x   cheaply. This bid by no means commits
   ♣ x x x x   you to spades as the trump suit. Partner
                                       will not assume you have more than four

cards in your suit and will not raise you (and agree that spades will
be trumps) unless he also has four cards. Remember four-card suits
are often bid to investigate for an eight-card fit. Of course, you will
not bid spades again on this hand, or bid anything at all, for that
matter, unless your partner shows enormous strength at his next turn.
But you are worth one response.

7. ♠ K J x x x   Things have improved a little. You would
   ♡ x x   certainly respond 1♠. And you might
   ◊ A x x   plan to bid some more later on.
   ♣ Q x x

8. ♠ A Q x x x   Even though you have a good hand and
   ♡ x   plan to make sure that at least a game con-
   ◊ A x x x   tract is reached, you should respond just
   ♣ K J x   1♠. There are two reasons why. First it
                               is safe to respond cheaply here because

---

**A NEW SUIT BID BY
RESPONDER IS FORCING.**

For our system to work smoothly, certain bids compel partner to keep
bidding. A double raise of opener's suit is one example of a forcing
bid; a new suit bid by responder is another. So don't be afraid that
partner will pass your 1♠ response. You respond cheaply to save
bidding space — you and partner will have plenty of room to search
for your best contract. (You know, when partner opens, that there
should be a game somewhere, but you don't know which game.) After
you hear partner bid one or two more times, hopefully you will know
where to place the contract.

So we see that responder can suggest a new suit *at the one level*
with as few as 6 points, but perhaps with a lot more. Now suppose
you have a suit to suggest, but to show it, you must go the two level.

64

9. ♠ A x x   To suggest a new suit at the two level
   ♡ x x   (increasing the level of the contract),
   ◊ Q x x   requires, as you might expect, a better
   ♣ K Q x x x   hand than a 6-point, minimum response.
                      We draw the line at about 10 points. With
                      this hand, bid 2♣.

10. ♠ x x x   You cannot respond 2♣ here; partner
   ♡ x x   would think you had more strength and
   ◊ K x x   might bid too much. But you must re-
   ♣ K J x x x   spond. The only option is to bid 1 NT.
                      A 1 NT response is a catch-all, negative
reply to an opening bid. It shows 6-9 points, but denies support for
partner's suit or a suit of your own that you could bid at the one
level. It says that you must bid something and 1 NT is all you can do.

11. ♠ K x x   Bid 1 NT. A 1 NT response doesn't
   ♡ x   promise a balanced hand. Sometimes you
   ◊ J x x   are forced to make this response, lacking
   ♣ K x x x x x   any other bid, even when your hand is un-
                      balanced.

12. ♠ K x x x   This time you have a suit you can show
   ♡ x x   at the one level, so the proper response
   ◊ K x x x   is 1♠.
   ♣ Q x x

13. ♠ A J x   A 2 NT response has a special meaning.
   ♡ x x x   The bid shows 13-15 high-card points,
   ◊ K x x   balanced pattern, and a "stopper," or
   ♣ K Q 10 x   sure trick, in all the unbid suits. This is
                      a forcing bid.

14. ♠ A J x   The meaning of a 3 NT response is easy to
   ♡ x x x   remember. You show a hand you would
   ◊ K Q x   have opened 1 NT had you been the open-
   ♣ A K x x   ing bidder, that is, 16-18 high-card points
                      and balanced pattern. (This bid is not
forcing — since game has been reached, partner can pass if he is
satisfied to stop in game.)

Responder has one other option at his first turn. This is a jump in a new suit, called a jump shift. This is a way responder can show strong interest in bidding a slam, so a jump shift shows a very powerful hand. (Remember that it is not necessary to jump in a suit if your hand is only fairly strong, since any new suit bid by responder is forcing. Look at hand #8 again.)

15. ♠ A K Q J x x
♥ Q x
♦ A x x
♣ x x

Your chances for slam are bright, so jump to 2♠ (and plan to bid spades again at your next turn, showing a really powerful suit.

16. ♠ A K x x x
♥ K J x x
♦ x
♣ A x x

You have an excellent fit for your partner's hearts as well as great strength, so you may be able to make a slam. Jump to 2♠ to alert partner to your interest in slam. (At your next turn, you will support his hearts.)

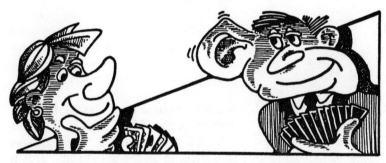

KEEP YOUR EAR OPEN FOR RESPONDER'S FIRST BID.

Let's review the options responder has in making his first bid:

RAISE partner to two, three or straight to game.
A raise to two shows 6-9 points and support.
A raise to three shows 13-15 points and four-card support.
A raise to game shows excellent support, a distributional hand, but fewer than 10 high-card points.

BID A NEW SUIT at the one or two level or with a jump.
A bid of a new suit at the one level shows 6 or more points and a suit at least four cards long.
A bid of a new suit at the two level shows at least 10 high-card points and a suit at least four cards long.
A jump bid in a new suit, called a *JUMP SHIFT,* shows a strong interest in slam. It shows a very powerful hand with a self-sufficient trump suit, strong support for partner's suit or an immensely powerful balanced hand — usually at least 17 points.

RESPOND IN NOTRUMP at the one, two or three level.
A 1 NT bid is a catch-all negative reply showing 6-9 high-card points, denying support for partner's suit and denying a suit that could be bid at the one level.
A 2 NT bid shows 13-15 high-card points, a balanced pattern and a stopper in all of the unbid suits.
A 3 NT bid shows the equivalent of an opening 1 NT bid — 16-18 high-card points and a balanced pattern with a stopper in all unbid suits.

With a sound knowledge of the bidding system, it is possible for you and partner to exchange much information. Learning the system may require some effort and memorization on your part, but your reward will be accurate contracts.

INTRODUCTION TO DEFENSIVE PLAY:
SECOND-HAND PLAY

We continue to discuss some of the elements of good defensive play. We saw how the defenders can help each other by the lead of an informative card. But suppose that *declarer* has led to the trick (either from his own hand or the dummy). What strategy should the defense adopt?

The first defender to play typically will play a waiting game by playing a low card. By doing so he may:

(1)   Make declarer guess what to play from his hand or dummy in third seat.
(2)   Force declarer to use a high card to prevent your partner, who gets to play last, from winning the trick with a low card.
(3)   Avoid the embarrassment of wasting one of his high cards on the same trick when his partner may be forced to play a high card.
(4)   Make it more difficult for declarer to establish tricks.

So the general rule for this situation is:

> ### SECOND HAND LOW.

Most of the time you will follow with a low card if you are second to play without giving the matter too much thought. Let's look at some example situations that illustrate how the rule works.

1.   x x
    Q 9 x x x   A 10 x x
               K J

Declarer needs one trick from this suit and leads from dummy. He will have no problem if East plays his ace. But if East plays low as second hand, declarer must guess what to do. He will be successful if he plays his king this time, but he will lose if he plays the jack. If East had the queen and West had the ace, declarer would have to play the jack from his hand to take one trick.

2.　　　　　　　　　　A 10 x
　　　Q x x

Declarer leads low toward the dummy. You should play low quickly. Don't even think about doing anything else. If declarer plays the
ten from dummy and your partner cannot beat it, then declarer has
the king and jack in his hand and you would have accomplished
nothing by playing your queen. Dismiss any thoughts of playing the
queen "to force out the ace." If you play low, there is a good chance
you will win a trick with your queen later.

3.　　　　　　　　　　A x x
　　　J x x　　　　　　　　　K x x
　　　　　　　Q 10 x x

Declarer attacks this suit by cashing the ace and leading low toward
his hand. East should play low, and declarer will have to guess
whether to play the queen or the ten from his hand. What we call
"table presence" is a factor in situations like this. Not only must
East play low on the second spade, he must manage to do so *without
pause for thought.* If East thinks for a long time before playing low,
declarer will know East has the king and was considering winning
the trick. And in bridge, declarer has the right to act on this information. (In case you are wondering, it would be very improper for
East to hesitate if he had the jack, deliberately trying to fool declarer.
In bridge, there is a strict code of ethics that prohibits sharp prac-
tices such as this.)

4.　　　　　　　　　　x x x
　　　J x x　　　　　　　　　A 10 x x
　　　　　　　K Q x

Declarer can always make two tricks here leading toward his hand
twice. If East plays his ace on the first lead of the suit, declarer has
his two tricks ready. If East ducks the first trick, declarer will have
to find a way to get to dummy so that he can lead toward his hand
a second time. So the defenders can make his task just a little more
awkward.

5.　　　　　　　　　　9 x x x
　　　K　　　　　　　　　　A x x x
　　　　　　　Q J 10 x

69

Declarer leads from dummy. East had better play low!

6.   A 9 x
    J x x
                      Q x x
              K 10 x x

Declarer leads low toward the dummy. If West makes the error of playing his jack, dummy wins and declarer leads low to his ten, finessing against East and bringing in this whole suit. This is a good example of how putting up a high card in second seat can be costly.

We have seen that it is often right to play low as second hand even if you can win the trick with a higher card. For example:

7.   Q x x
    K 10 x
                      A 9 x x
              J x x

Declarer leads a low card toward dummy. West must play low to prevent declarer from taking a late trick.

Now look at this example:

8.   Q x
    K J 9 x

If declarer leads low toward dummy in this position, West can afford to win. This is a case where winning the trick cannot be costly. So there are times when you can safely disregard the rule of "Second Hand Low." Look at this example:

9.   x x x

                      K Q J 9 x

Declarer leads low from dummy. Here, it makes sense to "split your honors," forcing declarer to use his ace if he wants to win this trick, and establishing some tricks for yourself. When you split your honors as a defender, in second position, play the top card in the sequence. This tells your partner that you have the card directly below the honor played.

There are other times to make an exception to the rule of Second Hand Low. Perhaps the most common time is when declarer leads a *high* card to the trick. In such a case, it may be right for you to cover with some higher card that you happen to hold. We will examine this proposition in a later chapter.

TEST YOUR COMPREHENSION OF THE MATERIAL IN THIS CHAPTER:

QUIZ ON RESPONDING TO THE OPENING BID:

I. Partner has opened 1 ♠. What do you respond with:

1. ♠ Jxxx
   ♡ Qxx
   ◊ Jxx
   ♣ xxx

2. ♠ Kxxx
   ♡ Axx
   ◊ xx
   ♣ Jxxx

3. ♠ Jxx
   ♡ xx
   ◊ AQxxx
   ♣ xxx

4. ♠ KQxx
   ♡ xx
   ◊ AQxx
   ♣ Kxx

5. ♠ AQxxx
   ♡ —
   ◊ xxx
   ♣ J10xxx

6. ♠ xx
   ♡ AKxxx
   ◊ xx
   ♣ Jxxx

7. ♠ AK
   ♡ xx
   ◊ Qxxxx
   ♣ Qxxx

8. ♠ x
   ♡ Qxx
   ◊ Qxxxxx
   ♣ Kxx

9. ♠ xx
   ♡ A10x
   ◊ KJxx
   ♣ AQxx

II. Partner has opened 1 ♣. What do you respond with:

1. ♠ Axx
   ♡ xx
   ◊ xxxx
   ♣ KJxx

2. ♠ xx
   ♡ Jxx
   ◊ Qxxxx
   ♣ Axx

3. ♠ Axx
   ♡ xx
   ◊ Axx
   ♣ KQxxx

4. ♠ xxx
   ♡ KJxx
   ◊ xxx
   ♣ Qxx

5. ♠ Kxxxx
   ♡ AQxx
   ◊ Jx
   ♣ xx

6. ♠ Kxxx
   ♡ Qxxx
   ◊ Axx
   ♣ xx

7. ♠ AJxxx
   ♡ Kxxxx
   ◊ xx
   ♣ x

8. ♠ AKxx
   ♡ Kxxxx
   ◊ xx
   ♣ Ax

9. ♠ xxx
   ♡ Kxxx
   ◊ xx
   ♣ AQxx

10. ♠ AQx
    ♡ KJxx
    ◊ xxx
    ♣ Kxx

11. ♠ AQx
    ♡ Kxx
    ◊ K10xx
    ♣ Qxx

12. ♠ xx
    ♡ AKJxx
    ◊ Ax
    ♣ KQxx

III. With each of these hands, give the correct response to an opening bid in each of the four suits.

1. ♠ x
   ♡ Q10xxxx
   ◊ Kxx
   ♣ Qxx

2. ♠ xx
   ♡ AQxx
   ◊ KJxx
   ♣ K10x

3. ♠ xx
   ♡ AKxx
   ◊ xxx
   ♣ AQxx

4. ♠ Ax
   ♡ Qxxx
   ◊ xxx
   ♣ KQxx

5. ♠ AQ
   ♡ Jxxx
   ◊ Jxxx
   ♣ xxx

SOLUTIONS:

I. 1. Pass
    2, 2♠.
    3. 2♠. Raise partner's major whenever possible to establish the major suit fit. You aren't strong enough to bid 2◊ anyway.
    4. 3♠
    5. 4♠
    6. 1 NT. Not strong enough to bid 2♡.
    7. 2◊
    8. 1 NT. No choice.
    9. 2 NT

II. 1. 2♣
    2. 1◊
    3. 3♣
    4. 1♡
    5. 1♠, your longest suit.
    6. 1♡. With two four-card majors, bid the lower. If partner has four-card support for your suit, he will raise. If, instead, he has four spades, he will bid 1♠ and you will raise.
    7. 1♠. Bid the higher ranking of two long suits, both of which you plan to bid, just as in opening the bidding.
    8. 1♡. Good hand, but you can afford to go slow.

9. 1 ♡   Show the major suit. Finding a fit in a major suit is your first goal because you score more points if playing with a major suit as trumps. Also, game at a major suit is available for only ten tricks.
10. 1 ♡
11. 2 NT
12. 2 ♡

III. 1. 1 ♣ - 1 ♡   2. 1 ♣ - 1 ♡*   3. 1 ♣ - 1 ♡
      1 ◊ - 1 ♡   1 ◊ - 1 ♡   1 ◊ - 1 ♡
      1 ♡ - 4 ♡   1 ♡ - 3 ♡   1 ♡ - 3 ♡
      1 ♠ - 1 NT   1 ♠ - 2NT   1 ♠ - 2 ♣

      4. 1 ♣ - 1 ♡   5. 1 ♣ - 1 ♡*
      1 ◊ - 1 ♡   1 ◊ - 1 ♡
      1 ♡ - 2 ♣**   1 ♡ - 2 ♡
      1 ♠ - 2 ♣   1 ♠ - 1 NT

  * When you respond to a 1 ♣ opening bid with four diamonds and four hearts, bid 1 ♡ to try to immediately locate an eight-card fit in the major suit.
** You cannot raise hearts because no immediate raise shows your point count accurately. 2 ♡ shows 6-9, 3 ♡ shows 13-15. So you must *temporize* with 2 ♣ (a new suit bid at the two level, which shows at least 10 points), and raise hearts at your next turn.

QUIZ ON SECOND-HAND PLAY:

1.   7 5 3
                              You
                        K J 9 2
Declarer leads this suit from dummy. Which card do you play?

2.   K 10
      You
      Q J 9 8
Declarer leads low toward dummy. Which card do you play?

3.   K 7 5 2
      You
      A Q J 8
Declarer leads low toward dummy. Which card do you play?

4.   Q 10 3
                        You
                        A J 5
Declarer leads low from dummy. Which card do you play?

5.   A 7 5
                        You

                        K 8 2
Declarer plays the ace and then leads low from dummy. Which card
do you play?

6.   A J 8
        You
        K Q 4
Declarer leads low toward dummy. Which card do you play?

SOLUTIONS:

1. Play the deuce. If declarer has the AQ10 and he is about to
    finesse his ten, there is nothing you can do about it. You have
    no reason to do anything but wait.
2. Play the queen, just in case declarer is thinking about playing
    the ten from dummy.
3. Play the ace. You won't help declarer any by going ahead and
    winning this trick (since you have all the other intermediates
    in this suit). And there is a danger that you won't get your ace
    if you don't take it now — declarer could have a singleton.
4. Play the five. If declarer has, say, K9xx, you will help him
    by playing either the jack or ace. Play low and you may take
    tricks with both your jack and ace.
5. Play low. Declarer has Q10xx. He will have to guess whether
    to play his queen or his ten. In a situation like this, where
    declarer may be faced with a guess, you must make up your
    mind to play low in second seat ahead of time, so that when
    the crucial moment arrives, you can follow without thinking
    about it. If you do this, declarer won't be able to tell that you
    have the king and could have won the trick if you wanted to.
6. Play the four, unless you want to make sure that your side gets
    one trick, in which case you would "split your honors." If you
    play low, declarer might play the eight from dummy (it would
    be his correct play if he had 10xx or 9xx), and your partner
    will win a surprise trick with his nine or ten.

Chapter 5

OPENER'S REBID

In our bidding system, many different kinds of hands may be opened with the same bid. If, for example, opener bids 1 ◊ , he could have 11 or 12 high-card points or he could have 20 or more. Similarly, responder may not be able to show the strength of his hand or all of its features with his first bid. When the auction begins with one of a suit, it may take several bids before the partnership can place the contract.

This chapter deals with OPENER'S REBID. Assume you have opened the bidding with one of a suit, and partner has responded to your opening in some way. Now you must decide whether you should bid some more, and if so, what bid you should make. *Judgment* becomes a factor.

Opener bases his choice on how much he knows about responder's hand. There are two general cases to consider.

(CASE ONE) If responder has made a bid that tells how much strength he has, all opener has to do is add his point-count to the points responder showed, arrive at a total, and decide at what level the partnership should play. (Remember that if opener's suit is raised, his long cards may improve in value.) So, when responder limits his hand in some way at his first turn, it is up to opener to be the "captain" of the partnership. Let's look at some example auctions that illustrate this simple type of situation:

Suppose you have opened 1 ♠ and partner has raised to 2 ♠. He has 6-9 points in support of your suit, plus some help in spades, at least three cards. Here is what you should do holding each of the following hands:

1.	♠ A K x x x ♡ A x x ◊ K x ♣ x x x	Pass. You have 24 points at most so game is unlikely. Eight tricks may be all you can make.
2.	♠ A K J x x ♡ A x x ◊ A K x ♣ x x	Bid 4 ♠. You have 26 points at least, so there will be a good chance to make game. Do not make a lesser bid when you know the values for a game contract are available.

75

3. ♠ A Q x x x   You should have a game, with your
   ♡ Q 10 x   20-point hand opposite partner's 6-9. Bid
   ◊ A Q   3 NT, giving him the option of playing
   ♣ K Q x   game in notrump if his hand is balanced.
                  He can always return to spades.

4. ♠ K Q x x x   This time you are uncertain what to do.
   ♡ A x x   You have a hand worth about 17 points,
   ◊ A J x   so there is a chance for game, but only
   ♣ Q x   if partner has 8 or 9 points. Since it all
                  depends on him, you must ask him to
evaluate his raise. Bid 3 ♠. This bid is invitational to game. (If you
knew there was no chance for game, you would not bid any more
at all.) Partner will look at his hand again and decide whether his
2 ♠ bid is closer to minimum (6-7) or maximum (8-9). He will either
pass or go on to 4 ♠.

   You opened 1 ♣, but partner responded 1 NT. He has 6-9 points
but denies spade support.

5. ♠ A K x x x   Game is impossible and you have no
   ♡ K x x   reason to think there is any better contract
   ◊ Q x   than 1 NT. Pass, with your balanced
   ♣ Q x x   hand.

6. ♠ K Q J x x x   Bid 2 ♠. You have no interest in game,
   ♡ x   but you prefer to get out of notrump with
   ◊ Q x x   shortness in hearts and your long suit.
   ♣ A x x   Rebid it as cheaply as possible.

7. ♠ K Q J x x x   Hand #6 with the addition of the ◊ A.
   ♡ x   With an extra trick in hand, you make a
   ◊ A Q x   stronger rebid. Bid 3 ♠. If opener jumps
   ♣ A x x   in his own suit, he shows 15-18 high-card
                  points and a good six-card or longer suit.
                  Responder is encouraged to bid a game.

8. ♠ A K x x x   No interest in game, but it would be
   ♡ x x   wrong·to stay in notrump with this hand.
   ◊ x x   You have another suit to show. Bid 2 ♣
   ♣ A Q x x   and give partner a choice.

9. ♠ K Q J x x   You have the values for a game contract
   ♡ A x x   and 3 NT looks right with your balanced
   ◊ K Q J   hand. Do not bid less when you know that
   ♣ A x   there is a game.

10. ♠ K Q J x x   Hand #9 without the ♡A. Your hand is
   ♡ J x x   worth about 18 points so game is possible
   ◊ K Q J   if partner has closer to 9 points than 6.
   ♣ A x   Raise to 2 NT. This is invitational to game
                        and asks partner to make the final
                        decision.

11. ♠ A K x x x   You could bid 3 NT, but that isn't quite
   ♡ A x   right here because your hand isn't
   ◊ Q x   balanced. You have another suit. With this
   ♣ A Q x x   much strength, you show your other suit
with a jump to 3♣. A jump shift by
opener says there is a game somewhere for sure. Responder must
keep bidding.

12. ♠ Q 10 x x x   You opened 1♠ and partner responded
   ♡ A x x   2 NT. That shows 13-15 points, balanced
   ◊ K J x   pattern, and some high cards in all the
   ♣ A x   unbid suits. You are forced to bid on, and
                        the obvious thing to do is raise to 3 NT.
If partner had responded 3 ♠ showing 13-15 points and good spade
support, at least four cards, you would go on to 4♠ , since partner's
double raise is forcing.

13. ♠ K J 10 x x   Partner responded 3 NT to your 1♠ open-
   ♡ Q x   ing. He has a balanced 16-18 points. This
   ◊ A x x   is easy as pie. Your 17 plus your partner's
   ♣ A K x   16-18 give you a total of 33-35 high-card
                        points. You can bid 6 NT confidently.
Don't be afraid to leap all the way to six. That's what your cards
are worth.

Notice that in each of these examples, responder's first bid was
limited as to strength. Opener could take over and place the contract
directly or invite a game.

(CASE TWO) Now suppose that responder bids *a new suit* at his first turn. A response in a new suit promises at least 6 points if made at the one level, at least 10 points if made at the two level. Of course, responder could have a lot more than 6 points or 10 points and still choose to make his first bid at the cheapest possible level, as we have seen. If you open 1♣ and your partner's hand is:

♠ A Q x x x
♡ A J x x
◊ K J x
♣ x

he will bid just 1♠ (forcing) at his first turn, saving room to allow your side to look around for the best contract. Another thing: if partner responds 1♠ to a 1♣ opening, you know he has at least four spades. But he could have five or six or more cards, and his suit could be good or bad. The point of all this is that opener cannot hope to place the contract accurately — he just doesn't have enough information. In this case, opener will *make some further bid that describes his own hand to responder.* Opener will try to clarify what type of hand he has (balanced, unbalanced, maximum, minimum, etc.) hoping that responder may be able to place the contract accurately if he hears more.

Suppose you have opened 1◊ and your partner responded 1♠. Let's look at some possible rebids. Many of them are just common sense:

1. ♠ A K
    ♡ x x
    ◊ K Q x x x x
    ♣ J x x

2◊. This shows a minimum, no more than 15 high-card points, and long diamonds. You will often have a six-card suit or longer. Do not consider raising spades, even though you have the top honors. Partner could have only a four-card spade suit when he suggests spades as trumps — the enemy would have more trumps than your side!

2. ♠ A K
    ♡ x x
    ◊ K Q 10 x x x
    ♣ A J x

3◊. This hand is about a trick better than the first one. If opener jumps in his own suit, he has 15-18 high-card points and a good six-card or longer suit. Responder is encouraged to bid again, but may pass with a minimum, 6-point response.

3. ♠ x x   **2♣**. You can suggest another possible
   ♡ Q x   trump suit. There is no reason why
   ◊ A K x x x   partner couldn't have some clubs (as well
   ♣ A J x x   as the spades he has already shown) and
                 if he does you will find your fit. Don't
rebid 2◊. If partner passes and puts down one diamond and four
clubs in dummy, you would be at fault for missing the best trump
suit. If you show your clubs, partner can always take you back to
diamonds if he thinks that suit will be better.

4. ♠ K x   **2♣**. This is an above-average hand, but
   ♡ x x   2♣ is all you can do. You aren't strong
   ◊ A K J x x   enough to jump to 3♣, which would say
   ♣ A Q x x   that you were confident of game once
                 partner was able to respond to your open-
ing. A simple change of suit can have a wide range in our system,
anywhere from 12-18 high-card points.

5. ♠ A x   On this monster, you can jump-shift to
   ♡ x x   **3♣**. Now that you know partner has at
   ◊ A K x x x   least six points, you want to bid a game
   ♣ A K Q x   somewhere. Over your jump shift, part-
                 ner has to keep going; he can prefer
                 diamonds, raise clubs, rebid his spades or
                 try notrump.

6. ♠ J x x x   **2♠**. Partner has at least four spades, so
   ♡ x x   you have found a home . This is a mini-
   ◊ A K J x   mum opening, so all you do is raise him
   ♣ A x x   one level. Notice that you raise the spades,
                 where your side is known to have a great
many cards, rather than rebid your good diamonds. In picking out
a trump suit, *length* is the most important consideration. You would
avoid a spade raise here with less than four-card support, since partner might have only four spades.

7. ♠ Q J x x   **3♠**. 16-18 points in support of spades and
   ♡ x x   four-card support. Partner is urged to go
   ◊ A K Q x x   on to four unless he has a very minimum
   ♣ A x   response.

8. ♠ K Q x x
    ♡ Q x
    ◊ A K Q x x
    ♣ A x

With this hand, you can bid 4♠. Even if partner has only six points and only four spades for his response, you are prepared to play in game, and that is what your bid says. If partner happens to have a good hand, he can certainly bid some more.

9. ♠ Q x x
    ♡ K x x
    ◊ A Q x x
    ♣ K x x

Bid 1 NT. If you have a balanced, minimum opening, you can describe it to partner by opening in your longest suit and, rebidding the cheapest number of notrump at your second turn.

10. ♠ Q x
    ♡ K x x
    ◊ A Q x x x
    ♣ K x x

You could rebid 2 ◊ here, since it is permissible to rebid any five-card suit but a 1 NT rebid is more descriptive with your balanced hand and points in every suit.

11. ♠ x x
    ♡ x x x
    ◊ A K Q x x
    ♣ A x x

This time you would rebid your strong five-card suit.

12. ♠ K x
    ♡ A Q x
    ◊ K Q 10 x x
    ♣ A J x

Jump to 2 NT. This is how to show a balanced hand a little too strong for a notrump opening. You open one of a suit and skip one level in notrump at your next turn to bid. You suggest 19-20 high-card points and a balanced pattern. Partner will almost always go on, but he is allowed to pass if he has really scraped up a response to your opening bid.

13. ♠ K x x
    ♡ A Q x
    ◊ K Q 10 x
    ♣ A K x

With another point, you could have opened 2 NT. Now that partner has responded to 1 ◊, you must make sure game is reached. The best action is to jump all the way to 3 NT.

To review, there are several ways opener can continue to describe his hand if responder bids a new suit at his first turn. He can rebid the same suit he opened, try another suit, raise responder's suit or bid notrump. He can rebid cheaply with a minimum hand or jump to show extra strength.

OPENER'S REBID — after an opening suit bid and a response:

There are several options:
CASE ONE — If responder has made a bid that *limits his strength:*

PASS —	if you know no game contract is possible and you are satisfied with the contract.
TRY TO IMPROVE THE CONTRACT —	if partner responds 1 NT, you may suggest another suit if your hand looks unsuitable for notrump.
TRY FOR GAME —	if responder has limited his hand in some way and there may be a game depending on whether he is in the minimum or maximum range for his bidding.
FORCE TO GAME —	by jumping in a new suit.
BID GAME —	if you know the values for game are present and which game contract is best.

*WE'RE SURE YOU KNOW
ALL THE RULES BY NOW!*

CASE TWO — If responder bids *a new suit:* opener must describe his hand further —

REBID THE MINIMUM NUMBER OF NOTRUMP — with 13-15 high-card points and balanced pattern. This bid denies another suit you can show at the one level or four-card support for the suit your partner showed.

JUMP ONE-LEVEL IN NOTRUMP — with 19-20 and balanced pattern.

JUMP TO 3 NT — with 21 points and a balanced pattern.

RAISE PARTNER'S SUIT ONE LEVEL — with 13-15 points and four-card support (rarely, three-card support).

RAISE PARTNER'S SUIT TWO LEVELS — with 16-18 points and four-card support.

RAISE PARTNER'S SUIT TO GAME — with 19 or more points and four-card support.

If you hold a second suit of four or more cards —

BID YOUR SECOND SUIT — as cheaply as possible with 13-18 points.

JUMP IN YOUR SECOND SUIT — with 19 points or more. This bid, a jump shift, is forcing (to game).

If you hold just one long suit —

REBID YOUR LONG SUIT — as cheaply as possible with 13-15 points.

JUMP IN YOUR LONG SUIT — with 16-18 points and a good six- or seven-card suit.

In theory, you may REBID any suit of five or more cards. Avoid rebidding a suit of only five cards, however, if there is an alternative. Rebid in notrump if your hand is balanced or show another suit if you have one.

We saw that a defender who is second to play to a trick usually adopts the strategy of *waiting*. He plays a low card and lets declarer, who plays from his own hand or dummy next, decide what to do. There is one important exception to this rule. Say that declarer leads not a low card but a high one. In such a case, it might be right for the defender in second seat to cover declarer's lead with a higher card of his own. The effect of this play will be to make declarer spend two of his high cards to win just one trick, and some lower intermediate card the defenders hold may be promoted. So it may be correct to

| COVER AN HONOR WITH AN HONOR. |

This example shows how covering an honor can gain:

```
              Q x
9 x x x                    K x x
              A J 10 x
```

If declarer leads the queen from dummy, East must cover with the king to establish a trick for his side. If he does not, declarer will pass the queen. Next, he leads low to his jack. Finally, the ace fells East's king, and the ten is high. Four tricks for declarer. But if East covers the queen, West's nine will control the fourth round of the suit, declarer having had to spend both his ace and queen on the first trick.

```
              J x
9 x x x                    Q x x
              A K 10 x
```

If declarer leads the jack, covering with the queen will gain a trick.

```
              10 x
Q 9 x                      K x x
              A J x x x
```

This is a common situation. Declarer leads the ten from dummy. If East plays low, declarer passes the ten to West's queen. Later, he can lead from dummy to his jack and take four tricks. But if East covers the ten, no matter how declarer plays the defenders get two tricks.

$$J x$$
$$10 \; x \; x \; x \qquad\qquad A \; x$$
$$K \; Q \; x \; x \; x$$

Declarer leads the jack from dummy. This example is slightly different. If East wins the jack with the ace, West's ten will be promoted. If East ducks, the jack wins. Declarer leads dummy's low card next and East has to play his ace, capturing nothing but low cards. It is a little harder for the East player to go right in this situation — when dummy's jack is led, there is a temptation to play low, hoping declarer is about to take a finesse, losing to West's hoped-for queen.

If declarer leads an unsupported honor from dummy, covering often will gain a trick. Remember the basis for this rule. You hope that by covering and forcing declarer to spend two of his high cards on the same trick, you may be able to promote some of your side's intermediate cards. Would you cover an honor in this situation?

$$Q \; J \; 10 \; 9$$
$$K \; x \; x \; x$$

Declarer leads the queen from dummy. Clearly, you should not play your king here. Your side has no intermediate cards to promote — you can see them all in dummy!

Suppose clubs are trumps, declarer having bid and rebid the suit. Dummy turns up with Jxx of clubs and you hold Qxx. At some point, declarer leads the ♣J. Should you cover? Of course not. There is nothing to gain. With declarer known to have at least five clubs for his bidding, your side holds no intermediate cards to promote. Make up your mind in advance that you will be ready to play low neither too quickly nor too slowly if declarer leads the ♣J from dummy.

What we call *table presence* is a factor here. If you produce a low club on dummy's jack, looking as though you have not a care in the world, declarer may decide you don't have the queen he is missing, and refuse to take the finesse. If you go into a long mull or even flinch at all, however, you will give away that you have the crucial card.

In the example situation above, dummy has such good intermediate

cards that covering cannot possibly gain. But suppose dummy's holding is not quite so good.

	Q J 9	
10 x x		K x x x
	A x x	

Declarer leads the queen from dummy. Do you see what will happen if you cover? Declarer wins the ace, and dummy remains with the J9 (a holding we call a tenace). Declarer can now lead from his hand and finesse your partner's ten successfully, bringing in three tricks. But suppose you refuse to cover the queen. *If the jack is led next, you cover*, hoping that your partner does have the ten. (If declarer has the ten, there is nothing you can do.)

There is a good rule for those situations where dummy has a broken sequence and declarer leads from dummy. Wait until the last card in the sequence is led before covering. Here's another illustration of how this can gain:

<pre>
                  J 10 x
   K 9 x x   Q x x
                  A x x
</pre>

Declarer attacks this suit by leading the jack from dummy. You must duck. If you cover, declarer wins and leads back toward dummy's ten. Your partner will be unable to prevent declarer from winning two tricks. If you duck, declarer passes the jack to partner's king. Later you will cover the ten. If your partner has the nine, you will promote a trick by covering the second time. Again, if declarer has the nine, you can do nothing, so you might as well assume partner holds that card.

So far, dummy has been the hand to lead. The defenders could plainly see what intermediate cards dummy had. Deciding whether it is best to cover an honor that declarer leads *from his hand* can be very difficult.

<pre>
                  A 10 x
   Q x x
</pre>

Declarer leads the jack from his hand. Do you cover with your queen? The answer depends on what declarer has. If the layout is:

<pre>
                  A 10 x
   Q x x   K 9 x x x
                  J x
</pre>

you will save a trick by covering. (Work it out.) But if the situation is:

<pre>
                  A 10 x
   Q x x   x x
                  K J 9 x x
</pre>

it is obvious that covering will give declarer the entire suit. Generally, declarer will have a good holding in any suit he attacks promptly. So you should probably duck (smoothly) here. Very few declarers will lead the jack in this situation holding only Jx. Of course, if declarer has bid this suit, you would know not to cover.

TEST YOUR COMPREHENSION OF THE MATERIAL IN THIS CHAPTER.

QUIZ ON OPENER'S REBID:

I. You open 1 ♡, partner responds 1 ♠. What do you rebid with:

1. ♠ Qx
   ♡ AQxxx
   ◊ Kxx
   ♣ QJx

2. ♠ x
   ♡ AQxxx
   ◊ Kxxx
   ♣ AJx

3. ♠ x
   ♡ QJxxxx
   ◊ Axx
   ♣ AQx

4. ♠ Jxxx
   ♡ AKJxx
   ◊ Ax
   ♣ xx

5. ♠ Kx
   ♡ AKJxx
   ◊ A10x
   ♣ KJx

6. ♠ Ax
   ♡ AKJxx
   ◊ xx
   ♣ AKJx

7. ♠ Ax
   ♡ AKJxxx
   ◊ KQx
   ♣ xx

8. ♠ AKxx
   ♡ AKxxx
   ◊ Qx
   ♣ xx

9. ♠ Kx
   ♡ AKQxxxx
   ◊ AQ
   ♣ xx

10. ♠ AKxx
    ♡ AKxxx
    ◊ Ax
    ♣ Qx

II. You open 1 ♠, partner responds 2 ♣. What do you rebid with:

1. ♠ AKxxx
   ♡ xx
   ◊ Qxxx
   ♣ AQ

2. ♠ AKJxx
   ♡ AJxxx
   ◊ x
   ♣ xx

3. ♠ AKQxx
   ♡ xxx
   ◊ Ax
   ♣ Jxx

4. ♠ AQxxx
   ♡ QJx
   ◊ A10x
   ♣ Jx

5. ♠ AKxxx
   ♡ Ax
   ◊ xx
   ♣ Qxxx

6. ♠ AKxxx
   ♡ AKQxx
   ◊ Kx
   ♣ x

7. ♠ AQJ10xx
   ♡ Axx
   ◊ KQx
   ♣ x

8. ♠ AKJxx
   ♡ KQx
   ◊ AJx
   ♣ Jx

9. ♠ AKxxx
   ♡ Ax
   ◊ xx
   ♣ AQxx

III. You open 1 ◊, partner responds with 2 ◊. What do you rebid with:

1. ♠ AKJx
   ♡ xx
   ◊ KJxx
   ♣ Kxx

2. ♠ xx
   ♡ Ax
   ◊ AKJxxx
   ♣ Kxx

3. ♠ Ax
   ♡ Qxx
   ◊ KQxxxx
   ♣ AJ

IV. You opened 1 ◊, partner responds 3 ◊. What do you rebid with:

1. ♠ Kxx
   ♡ QJx
   ◊ AJxxx
   ♣ Kx

2. ♠ x
   ♡ Axx
   ◊ AJxxxx
   ♣ Kxx

3. ♠ x
   ♡ AKx
   ◊ KQxxxx
   ♣ AJx

V. You open 1 ◊, partner responds 1 NT. What do you rebid with:

1. ♠ Jx
   ♡ KJx
   ◊ AKxxx
   ♣ Qxx

2. ♠ x
   ♡ Axx
   ◊ KJxxxx
   ♣ Axx

3. ♠ x
   ♡ Axx
   ◊ KQJxxx
   ♣ AQx

4. ♠ Ax
   ♡ Jxx
   ◊ AKQxxx
   ♣ Qx

SOLUTIONS:

I.
1. 1 NT
2. 2 ◊
3. 2 ♡
4. 2 ♠
5. 2 NT
6. 3 ♣
7. 3 ♡
8. 3 ♠
9. 4 ♡
10. 4 ♠

II.
1. 2 ◊
2. 2 ♡
3. 2 ♠
4. 2 NT
5. 3 ♣
6. 3 ♡
7. 3 ♠
8. 3 NT
9. 4 ♣

III.
1. Pass
2. 3 ◊
3. 3 NT

IV.
1. 3 NT
2. 5 ◊
3. 6 ◊

V.
1. Pass
2. 2 ◊
3. 3 ◊
4. 2 NT

88

QUIZ ON COVERING HONORS:

1.   ♡ Q x

                    ♡ K x x x

Hearts is trumps, declarer having bid and rebid the suit. Do you cover if the queen is led?

2.   ♡ J x

                    ♡ K 10 9

The contract is notrump. Do you cover if the jack is led?

3.   ♡ J 10 9 x

                    ♡ Q 8 x x

The contract is notrump. Do you cover if the jack is led?

4.   ♣ 10 9

                    ♣ K J x

The contract is notrump. If declarer leads from dummy, do you put up one of your honors?

5.   ♠ K 10 9 8

 ♠ Q x x

The contract is notrump. Declarer leads the jack from his hand. Do you cover?

6.   ◊ 10 x

                    ◊ Q x

The contract is notrump. Declarer leads the ten from dummy. Do you cover?

SOLUTIONS:

1. No, you will make your king if you hold on to it, and there is no prospect of gain in covering.
2. Yes, you will promote your 109 by covering.
3. No, not with such strong intermediates in dummy.
4. Yes. This is a special case. Both you and dummy have *two* intermediates. If you cover both dummy's cards, you will promote a trick if declarer has AQxxx and partner holds 8xx.
5. No, all the intermediate cards are in dummy.
6. Yes, you might as well. Perhaps declarer has KJ8xx, leaving partner with A97x. You will gain by covering.

Chapter 6

RESPONDER'S REBID AND
PLACING THE FINAL CONTRACT

Contract bridge was invented in 1925. Before that, people played a different kind of bridge called auction bridge. There was bidding in auction bridge and there were game contracts. The big difference was that you got credit for making a game whether you bid it or not. Auction bridge has become nearly extinct, probably because the accuracy in the bidding that contract bridge demands makes it a much more challenging game.

Certain bids show a specific amount of strength. An opening bid of 1 NT or a single raise of an opening suit bid, in fact, show a narrowly-defined amount of strength. An important principle in the bidding is: *when one player has made a bid that shows how many points he has,* then *his partner becomes "captain" of the partnership and must see that the proper level is reached.*

An opening bid of 1 NT makes for a simple auction. Opener has described his strength and promised a tolerance for every suit, so responder can assume the captain's duties immediately. Auctions that begin with a bid of one of a suit, however, are often more complicated. If responder can raise opener's suit or bid notrump, he "limits his hand," another way of saying that he shows his point count, and opener can become captain. But if responder suggests a new suit at his first turn, the strength of his hand remains unlimited, and it is up to opener to try to limit *his* strength by making a second bid that is more descriptive of the hand he opened. Perhaps responder can become "captain" once he hears a little more about what opener has.

This brings us to RESPONDER's REBID. In discussing this part of the auction, we apply the following principle:

BY THE TIME RESPONDER HAS HEARD OPENER BID TWICE, HE WILL USUALLY HAVE ENOUGH INFORMATION TO PLACE THE CONTRACT.

Opener's rebid will usually limit his hand. For example, if opener begins with 1 ◊ and rebids 1 NT over a 1 ♡ response, he shows 13-15 points. Notice that opener's hand, on this sequence of bids, is also limited as to a possible trump suit. He cannot have four hearts, else he would have raised responder's suit, and he cannot have four spades, else he would have bid 1 ♠ instead of rebidding in notrump. Since responder will know by his second turn what the combined values of the partnership add up to (and quite possibly whether there is a good trump suit available), he will become captain. Let's look at some of the ways responder handles this:

Opener   *Responder*
1 ◊   1 ♡
1 NT

1. ♠ x
    ♡ Q 10 x x x x
    ◊ K x x
    ♣ Q x x

Bid 2♡. Game is impossible and you prefer to play in your long suit, especially when partner is known to have a tolerance for hearts. Remember, when opener rebids 1 NT, he shows either two or three hearts.

2. ♠ x
    ♡ A K x x x x
    ◊ K x x
    ♣ Q x x

Bid 4♡. You have enough strength for game and you have at least an eight-card heart fit. There is no reason to delay.

3. ♠ Q x x
    ♡ K x x x
    ◊ A x
    ♣ A J x x

Bid 3 NT. You have enough strength for game, and notrump looks fine.

4. ♠ A x x x
   ♡ K x x x
   ◊ 10 x
   ♣ K J x

Bid 2 NT. You may have a game in notrump, but only if opener has close to 15 points. A raise here is invitational to game and asks opener to make the final decision. There is no reason to bid spades since opener cannot have four of them.

5. ♠ x
   ♡ K x x x
   ◊ K J x x
   ♣ x x x x

Place the contract at 2 ◊. Game is impossible, but you much prefer to play this hand with partner's suit as trumps.

Opener	Responder
1 ♡	1 ♠
2 ♡	

6. ♠ A K x x
   ♡ Q x x
   ◊ A x x x
   ♣ x x

Bid 4 ♡. Opener shows a minimum opening bid with long hearts, so you know exactly where to play.

7. ♠ A K x x
   ♡ Q x x
   ◊ J x x x
   ♣ x x

Bid 3 ♡. This time you are only good enough to invite game. Opener has a minimum (13-15 points) and you want to be in game only if he has closer to 15. Your hand is worth about 11 points as dummy for a heart contract.

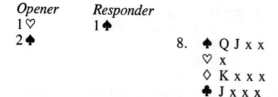

Opener	Responder
1 ♡	1 ♠
2 ♣	

8.　♠ Q J x x
　　♡ x
　　◊ K x x x
　　♣ J x x x

Pass. Partner has a minimum opening with four-card spade support. Lacking the strength for game, you can stop right here in what must be a good partscore contract.

9.　♠ A Q x x x
　　♡ x
　　◊ A x x x
　　♣ K x x

Bid 4 ♠.

Note that, in all the examples so far, opener made a minimum rebid which limited his strength to 13-15 points. Responder showed *weakness* by passing or signing off in a partscore; *invitational* values by making a second progressive-sounding bid, such as a raise; or *game-going strength* by placing the contract at game.

If opener makes a rebid that does not promise more than a minimum, responder:

```
SHOWS WEAKNESS.................with 6-9 points
INVITES GAMES ...................with 10-12 points
MAKES SURE GAME IS REACHED .......with 13 or
                                   more points
```

Let's look at another bidding sequence in which responder tries to place the contract based on what he knows after opener's rebid:

Opener	Responder
1 ◊	1 ♡
1 ♠	

Opener has shown length in spades and diamonds, at least four of each. He could have a fine hand, but maybe as few as 12 high-card points.

Suppose, to begin with, that responder is *weak* (6-9 points:

1. ♠ x x x x
   ♡ A Q x x
   ◇ x x
   ♣ x x x

   Pass. Game is unlikely and spades is a playable contract since you have at least eight trumps.

2. ♠ Q x x x
   ♡ A Q x x
   ◇ x x
   ♣ x x x

   Bid 2 ♠ showing 8 or 9 points and four-card trump support.

3. ♠ x x
   ♡ A Q x x
   ◇ x x x x
   ♣ x x x

   Even though you are as weak as before, it would be a mistake to pass with this hand. Take a *preference* to 2 ◇. You want to get back to your side's best trump suit.

4. ♠ x x
   ♡ K J x x
   ◇ Q x
   ♣ Q 10 x x x

   Bid 1 NT. A weak, balanced hand with no liking for either one of partner's suits.

5. ♠ x x
   ♡ K Q 10 x x x
   ◇ x x
   ♣ Q x x

   Bid 2 ♡, showing a weak hand; usually with at least six hearts.

Now let's give responder a little more strength (10-12 points), so that he knows game is possible, but only if opener has a little extra strength for his opening bid.

6. ♠ K Q x x
   ♡ A Q x x
   ◇ x x
   ♣ x x x

   Bid 3 ♠. Responder bids the limit of his values. 3 ♠ says, "Partner, I feel that 3 ♠ is a safe contract even if you have a very minimum opening. If you have a little extra, please bid game." Do not confuse this situation with an immediate double raise, which is forcing. Remember, at responder's *second* turn, he bids the limit of his hand.

95

7. ♠ x x
    ♡ K Q x x
    ◊ A Q x x
    ♣ x x x

Bid 3 ◊, inviting partner to bid again if he can. Do not make the mistake of bidding only 2 ◊ with this hand. A preference at the cheapest level is a weak action.

8. ♠ x x
    ♡ K Q x x
    ◊ x x x
    ♣ A Q x x

Bid 2 NT. "Partner, I'm willing to play this contract even if you have a minimum. If you have a little more, please bid again."

9. ♠ x x
    ♡ K Q J x x x
    ◊ A x
    ♣ J x x

Bid 3♡. Game in hearts is possible if partner can bid again.

Finally, suppose responder has an opening bid himself, so that he wants to reach a game contract for sure (regardless of what sort of opening bid his partner has).

10. ♠ A K x x
     ♡ K Q x x
     ◊ J x
     ♣ x x x

Bid 4♠.

11. ♠ Q x
     ♡ K Q x x
     ◊ x x x
     ♣ A Q 10 x

Bid 3 NT.

12. ♠ A x
     ♡ K Q J 10 x x
     ◊ Q x x
     ♣ x x

Bid 4♡. The ♡ 10, which makes this suit solid, is an important card.

13. ♠ A x
     ♡ K Q J x x
     ◊ x x
     ♣ A x x x

Bid 2♣, which forces partner to bid at least one more time. You must hear more before you can place the contract.

Let's list your options at RESPONDER'S REBID:

WITH WEAKNESS (6-9 points):	PASS, if you are willing to play right where you are. RAISE opener's second bid suit to the two level with 8 or 9 points and four-card trump support. TAKE A PREFERENCE to partner's first suit. REBID YOUR OWN SUIT CHEAPLY with a six-card suit or longer. BID 1 NT with a balanced hand and no four-card support for any suit bid by partner.
WITH INVITATIONAL VALUES (10-12 points):	RAISE partner's second suit to the three level or RAISE his first suit if he rebids it. TAKE A JUMP PREFERENCE to partner's first suit. JUMP REBID your own suit with a good six-card suit or longer. BID 2 NT.
WITH GAME-GOING VALUES (13 points or slightly more):	JUMP TO GAME IN ONE OF PARTNER'S SUITS, YOUR OWN SUIT OR NOTRUMP. BID A NEW SUIT to get more information.

Remember that this table of options assumes that opener has not shown extra strength at his second turn. If his rebid shows EXTRA STRENGTH, responder may bid game with correspondingly *less* strength.

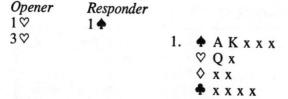

Opener   *Responder*
1♥   1♠
3♥

1. ♠ A K x x x
    ♥ Q x
    ◊ x x
    ♣ x x x x

Bid 4♥. Opener's jump shows 16-18 points and six or more good hearts. You have enough strength for game and Qx is adequate support when his suit is known to be excellent.

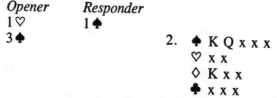

Opener   *Responder*
1♥   1♠
3♣

2. ♠ K Q x x x
    ♥ x x
    ◊ K x x
    ♣ x x x

Bid 4♠. Opener has shown 16-18 points and four-card spade support. Since your hand is worth about 9 points, you should be willing to try a game.

What would you bid in this situation?

Opener   *Responder*
1♥   2♥
3♥

3. ♠ A x x x
    ♥ K J x x
    ◊ x x x
    ♣ J x

Bid 4♥. Partner asked whether you had a minimum or a maximum raise and yours could hardly be better. Sometimes your job as responder will be to answer partner's questions about the value of your hand.

INTRODUCTION TO DEFENSIVE PLAY: THIRD-HAND PLAY

A couple of chapters ago, we learned that when declarer or dummy leads to a trick, the defender who is second to play will usually follow routinely with a low card. Now suppose that your *partner has led* to the trick, so that you are *third hand* to play. Here, the rule is exactly the opposite from the rule of second hand play. If third to play, you will usually need to play *high*.

The reason for this rule is seen in this illustration:

```
                6 5 4        You
     Q J 7 2                 K 9 3
                A 10 8
```

Partner led this suit. If he holds QJ102 or even QJ92, he would lead the queen, the top of his sequence. But as it is, he starts with his deuce, hoping you can contribute something to the trick that will help promote his intermediates. You must not disappoint him. Play your king.

The idea behind the rule of "Third Hand High" is that you are often willing to sacrifice a high card you hold in order to promote intermediate cards in your partner's hand. Suppose the layout is:

```
                6 5 4
     Q 10 7 2                K 9 3
                A J 8
```

You still play your king in third seat, and now your partner lurks with his queen-ten tenace behind declarer's jack. Notice that in both examples declarer will make an undeserved trick if you get cold feet and play your nine

```
                6 5 4
     J 8 7 2                 K 9 3
                A Q 10
```

Here, declarer has the ace-queen, but you still save a trick by playing your king. If your do not, declarer wins the ten and can finesse the queen successfully later.

```
                6 5 4
     Q 9 7 2                 A 10 3
                K J 8
```

If partner leads this suit, play your ace (and probably return partner's lead). Declarer will take only one trick with his king. He will make two tricks, however, if you fail to play your ace.

Sometimes you have *several* high cards of equal rank to choose from. For example:

```
                874
    K 6 5 2                     Q J 10
                A 9 3
```

Partner chooses to lead this suit. He leads the deuce, of course. If you play your queen and declarer wins, your partner will know his king is a winner, but he will not know that you have the jack and ten. Suppose you play the cheapest of your equals, the ten in this case. When your partner sees the ten force the Ace, he will know what is going on, won't he? He'll reason that declarer would not win the ace, setting up the king as a trick, if he could win with a lower card. So partner will know you must have the queen and jack as well as the ten.

When you *lead* to a trick in a suit headed by a sequence of cards, you lead the *top* card in your sequence. If you are *third* to play from a sequence, the rule is exactly the opposite. In third seat, you play the *bottom* card of equal high cards. This is another one of those little things the defenders do to overcome the handicap of not being able to see each other's cards.

```
                6 5 3
    K 9 7 4 2                   J played
                Q wins
```

Say that you are defending a notrump contract and your lead is the ◇4. The play goes: three, jack, queen. **Who has the Ace?** Declarer has it, right? Your partner would surely have played the ace if he held that card, helping you out as much as he could. **Now, who has the ten?** Declarer must have it. Partner would have played the ten, the cheaper card of his equals, if he had both the jack and ten. So we know declarer has AQ10(x). We cannot lead this suit again without giving declarer another trick with his ten.

There are exceptions to this rule of "Third Hand High," just as there are exceptions to most of the rules you will learn at bridge. Remember the idea the rule is based on: you are willing to sacrifice a high card if you can make declarer spend one of his high cards to win the trick and promote intermediate cards for your side. Look at this situation:

♡ Q J 10 9

♡ 2 led   ♡ K 5 4 3

Spades is trumps, and your partner has led the ♡2. Declarer is known to have the ace (remember that your partner would not underlead an ace against a suit contract. So you can accompish nothing by playing your king here. There are no intermediate cards to promote for your side; dummy has them all. Perhaps declarer has the singleton ace and will have to play it even if you play low.

A similar situation is:

♡ Q 7 4

♡ J 9 6 2   ♡ K 10 5

♡ A 8 3

Spades are trumps, and your partner has led the ♡2. Declarer is known to have the ace (remember that your partner would not underlead an ace against a suit contract.) So you can accomplish nothing by playing your king here. There are no intermediate cards to promote for your side; dummy has them all. Perhaps declarer has the singleton ace and will have to play it even if you play low.

♡ K 8 4

♡ 2 led   ♡ A J 6

Dummy plays low. Play your jack in third seat, hoping partner has led from the queen and you can win the trick without spending your ace.

♡ J 7 4

♡ 2 led   ♡ K 10 9

Spades is trumps. Dummy plays the four. With declarer known to have the ace, you must not play your king. Play the nine (cheaper of your equals). If the layout is this:

$$♡ J 7 4$$
$$♡ Q 6 5 2 \qquad\qquad ♡ K 10 9$$
$$♡ A 8 3$$

your nine will force the ace (and partner will know you have the ten when declarer fails to play it). If you were to play the king in this position, declarer would win the ace and make a trick with the jack later.

You will also save a trick by playing the nine if declarer's holding is AQx.

In the last few examples, the defender in third seat has essentially taken a *finesse* by playing a card that is not his highest! He hopes his partner, who has led to the trick, has a holding which will let the finesse work.

Let's look at one more example:

$$♡ A 10 4$$
$$♡ K 9 6 2 \qquad\qquad ♡ J 8 5$$
$$♡ Q 7 3$$

West leads the ♡2 against a spade contract, and dummy plays the four. East knows that declarer has at least one honor because West would lead the king if he had both the missing king and queen. So East plays the eight in third seat, saving a trick.

TEST YOUR COMPREHENSION OF THE MATERIAL IN THIS CHAPTER:

QUIZ ON RESPONDER'S REBID:

I.   Opener   Responder
   1♣   1♡
   1♠

1. ♠ x   2. ♠ xx   3. ♠ xx
   ♡ KJxx   ♡ AKxx   ♡ KQxx
   ◊ xxxx   ◊ KJxx   ◊ xxx
   ♣ Axxx   ♣ QJx   ♣ AQxx

4. ♠ AKxx   5. ♠ xx   6. ♠ Jxxx
   ♡ Jxxx   ♡ AJxx   ♡ Axxx
   ◊ xx   ◊ KJxx   ◊ Jx
   ♣ Kxx   ♣ Qxx   ♣ xxx

7. ♠ xx   8. ♠ xx   9. ♠ Ax
   ♡ KJxx   ♡ KQxxxx   ♡ AQJxxx
   ◊ KJxx   ◊ xx   ◊ xx
   ♣ xxx   ♣ Qxx   ♣ xxx

10. ♠ Ax   11. ♠ Kxxx   12. ♠ AQxx
   ♡ KQJ10xx   ♡ Axxx   ♡ AKxx
   ◊ Kxx   ◊ Jx   ◊ xx
   ♣ xx   ♣ xxx   ♣ Jxx

II. Opener   Responder
   1♣   1♠
   1 NT

1. ♠ AQ10xxx   2. ♠ Axxxx   3. ♠ KJxx
   ♡ xxx   ♡ x   ♡ Qxx
   ◊ Ax   ◊ xxx   ◊ AJxx
   ♣ xx   ♣ QJxx   ♣ xx

4. ♠ QJxx   5. ♠ Jxxxxx
   ♡ Axx   ♡ x
   ◊ Kx   ◊ Axxx
   ♣ Axxx   ♣ Qx

III. **Opener**   *Responder*
1 ♥   1 ♠
2 ♥

1. ♠ KJxx   2. ♠ AKxxx   3. ♠ KJxx
   ♥ x   ♥ Jxx   ♥ xx
   ♦ Axxx   ♦ Kx   ♦ AJxx
   ♣ xxxx   ♣ xxx   ♣ Qxx

4. ♠ AQxx   5. ♠ AKxx
   ♥ Qx   ♥ Qxx
   ♦ QJxx   ♦ Axxx
   ♣ KJx   ♣ xx

IV. **Opener**   *Responder*
1 ♦   1 ♠
2 ♠

1. ♠ AKxxx   2. ♠ AKxxx   3. ♠ Jxxx
   ♥ Kx   ♥ Kx   ♥ AJx
   ♦ Jxx   ♦ KJx   ♦ xxx
   ♣ xxx   ♣ xxx   ♣ KQx

V. **Opener**   *Responder*
1 ♥   1 ♠
3 ♥

1. ♠ KJxxx   2. ♠ AQxxx   3. ♠ KJxx
   ♥ Jx   ♥ Kx   ♥ xx
   ♦ Qx   ♦ xx   ♦ QJxx
   ♣ xxxx   ♣ xxxx   ♣ Kxx

VI. **Opener**   *Responder*
1 ♥   1 ♠
3 ♠

1. ♠ KJxx   2. ♠ KQxxx   3. ♠ Jxxx
   ♥ xx   ♥ xx   ♥ xx
   ♦ Qxxx   ♦ Axx   ♦ AJx
   ♣ Jxx   ♣ xxx   ♣ K10xx

VII. *Opener*   *Responder*
    1♡   2♡
    3♡

    1. ♠ Axx   2. ♠ Axx
       ♡ Qxx   ♡ Qxx
       ◊ xxx   ◊ xx
       ♣ Jxxx   ♣ Kxxxx

SOLUTIONS:

I.				II.			
	1.	2♣	(Weak)		1.	3♠	(Invitational)
	2.	3 NT	(Game bid)		2.	2♣	(Weak)
	3.	3♣	(Invitational)		3.	2 NT	(Invitational)
	4.	3♠	(Invitational)		4.	3 NT	(Game bid)
	5.	2 NT	(Invitational)		5.	2♠	(Weak)
	6.	Pass	(Weak)				
	7.	1 NT	(Weak)				
	8.	2♡	(Weak)				
	9.	3♡	(Invitational)				
	10.	4♡	(Game bid)				
	11.	2♠	(Weak)				
	12.	4♠	(Game bid)				

III.				IV.			
	1.	Pass	(Weak)		1.	3♠	(Invitational)
	2.	3♡	(Invitational)		2.	4♠	(Game bid)
	3.	2 NT	(Invitational)		3.	2 NT	(Invitational)
	4.	3 NT	(Game bid)				
	5.	4♡	(Game bid)				

V.			VI.		
	1.	Pass		1.	Pass
	2.	4♡		2.	4♠
	3.	3 NT		3.	3 NT

VII.			
	1.	Pass	(Rejecting the try for game)
	2.	4♡	(Accepting the try for game)

QUIZ ON THIRD-HAND PLAY:

I. In each problem, your partner has led the ♡2 against an opposing spade contract. You must decide what to play in third seat after dummy plays low.

1.
(Dummy)
♡ 7 5 3

♡2 led

(Your Hand)
♡ Q 9 6

2.
♡ J 7 4

♡2 led

♡ A 10 5

3.
♡ 9 6 4

♡ 2 led

♡ K J 5

4.
♡ K 6 4

♡2 led

♡ A J 5

5.
♡ 4 3

♡2 led

♡ J 10 9 8 7

6.   J9.72
♡ 8 6 4

♡2 led

♡ K Q 5

7.
♡ Q 7 5

♡ 2 led

♡ K J 10 9

8.
♡ Q J 10 9

♡ 2 led

♡ K 7 6 5 3

9.
♡ J 7 5

♡2 led

♡ K 10 6

10.
♡ Q 9 5

♡2 led

♡ K 10 8 4

II. Defending a contract of 1 NT, you lead a diamond from the ◊K9742. Dummy has three small diamonds. Partner plays the ◊J to trick one, and declarer wins the queen. Who has the ◊A? Who has the ◊10?

III. Defending a contract of 1 NT, you lead from the ♠K9642. Dummy has two small cards. Partner plays the ten to trick one and declarer wins the ace. Who has the jack? Who has the queen?

IV. Defending a contract of 1 NT, you lead from the ♡J9752. Dummy has two small cards. Partner plays the king at trick one, and declarer wins the ace. Who has the queen?

SOLUTIONS:

I.
1. Queen
2. Ace
3. King
4. Jack, hoping partner has led from the queen and you can win the trick without spending your ace.
5. Seven, the cheapest one of your equals.
6. Queen
7. Nine
8. Three. With declarer known to have the ♡A (since partner would not underlead that card against a suit contract), there is nothing to gain by playing your king.
9. Ten, hoping partner has led from the queen.
10. Eight, hoping partner has led from the jack.

II. Declarer has both the ◊A and ◊10. Partner would always play the ace if he had it, and would play the ten if he held both jack and ten.

III. Partner has both the jack and queen, since declarer did not win the trick with one of those cards instead of his ace.

IV. Declarer has the queen. Partner would play the cheaper card if he held both the king and queen.

Chapter 7

SOME EASY WAYS TO BID YOUR SLAMS

To bid and make a slam is an exciting accomplishment. As we will see when we talk about bridge scoring in detail, large bonuses are available for fulfilling slams. Even the bonus for a small slam is far greater than the points scored for making a game contract, and may be greater than the bonus for winning a *rubber,* which is the best two-out-of-three games. So accuracy in the bidding at the slam level is important. You have much to gain if your slam contract comes home, but if you bid a slam and go down, you lose not only a slam bonus but also the points you would have earned had you stopped at game.

When you bid a slam, you are contracting for 12 or 13 tricks. So you must have most of the strength in the deck. The two main factors to consider if you are thinking about a slam are:

(1) POWER —	You need a way to produce 12 or 13 tricks once the play gets started. About 33 points in high cards and distribution are needed for a small slam, about 37 for a grand slam. Your values may be primarily in aces and kings, or, if the contract is in a suit, you may have long suits and short suits to make up for what you lack in high cards.
(2) "CONTROLS" —	Your wealth of tricks will do you no good if the opponents can take two tricks before you get started. To make a slam, you must be able to prevent the defenders from defeating you outright — by winning two aces or an ace-king in the same suit.

There are many more things to consider in judging your slam prospects; for example, a shaky trump holding in a suit slam is a definite drawback. However, we will concentrate on the two main factors — POWER and CONTROLS.

The easiest slams to bid are those based on a straightforward evaluation of your high-card strength, your POWER. If your partner opens 1 NT and you hold a balanced 10 points, you can bid 3 NT with assurance. Many slams can be bid with exactly the same ease.

1. ♠ K x x   Partner opens 1 NT. Your side must have
    ♡ A x x   at least 33 high-card points, so you can bid
    ◊ A Q x x   6 NT without delay.
    ♣ K J x

If your hand is still better (this, unfortunately, won't happen very often):

2. ♠ K J x   Opposite a 1 NT opening, you can bid
    ♡ A Q x   7 NT, knowing that the high-card power
    ◊ A Q x x   for that contract is in hand.
    ♣ K Q x

For some reason, many players are reluctant to leap from 1 NT all the way to the six or seven level. You should view a hand like this as a great opportunity to be grasped. So do what you know is right. Always bid the values of your hand!

3. ♠ A x x   Here, there may be a slam, but only if
    ♡ K x x   partner has more than a minimum 16-
    ◊ A Q x x   point 1 NT opening. Remember that you
    ♣ K x x   need 33 points to bid slam (in this in-
                        stance, when you plan to bid slam in
notrump, in high cards alone) and you might have only 32. What is needed is a way to invite partner to bid a slam with a maximum holding. To invite a game in notrump, you raise a 1 NT opening to 2 NT. To invite a slam, you raise notrump past game to 4 NT. Logically, such a bid must show interest in slam. You would not bid 4 NT just to play that contract, since there is no bonus for getting to 4 NT and making it.

Over your 4 NT, partner will have to look at his hand again and decide whether to go on. He should pass with 16 points, bid 6 NT with 18, and use his judgment with 17.

Notice that on the first three examples, CONTROL of every suit was not a problem. You knew all suits were under control because your side had so much POWER. In the last example, if partner accepts your invitation to slam, he will have at least 17 points, so the opponents cannot have two aces to cash and are unlikely to have an ace-king in the same suit.

There are other bidding sequences in which you will be satisfied that CONTROLS are no problem and you may be able to bid a slam based strictly on POWER.

4. ♠ A Q x x x
   ♡ A J x x
   ◊ A x
   ♣ K x

Opener (You)	Responder
1♠	3♠

Bid 6♠. Your hand is worth about 20 points, and your partner shows 13-15 for his double raise. Good trumps and controls are not a problem, so you can leap to a slam.

5. ♠ K J 10 x x
   ♡ Q x x
   ◊ A x
   ♣ A x x

Opener	Responder (You)
1◊	1♠
2 NT	

Bid 6 NT. Opener has 19-20 points with balanced pattern so you can just jump to the right number of notrump.

6. ♠ A J 10 x x x
   ♡ A J x
   ◊ K x
   ♣ x x

Opener (You)	Responder
1♠	3♣
3♠	4♠

Now that spades have been raised, your hand is worth about 17 points, and responder, who has jump-shifted suggesting slam should have no fewer than 17 himself. Controls are no problem, since it is inconceivable that responder has an aceless hand. Bid 6♠.

7. ♠ A Q x x x
   ♡ A x
   ◊ Q x
   ♣ x x x x

Opener	Responder (You)
1◊	1♠
4♠	

Opener has shown 20 points and four-card spade support. Responder's hand is worth about 14. So he should jump to 6♠.

8. ♠ K x   *Opener (You)*   *Responder*
    ♡ A Q x x x   1♡   3♡
    ◇ A x x
    ♣ A x x

You might have a slam, but not if responder has raised with a 13-point minimum. Bid 5♡, inviting him to continue if his double raise is better than minimum. Partner should realize that you are interested in slam when you voluntarily go past game.

CONTROLS have not been a problem in any of these examples. The opponents could not defeat you in slam by taking two fast tricks. This will not always be the case, however. Sometimes you must be sure that all suits are under control before you can bid a slam, even if you have ascertained that you have the necessary power.
Look at this auction:

Opener   *Responder*
1♠   2♣
3♠   6♠

The two hands were:

Opener   *Responder*
♠ A Q J 10 x x   ♠ K x x
♡ K x   ♡ A x x x
◇ K Q J x   ◇ x
♣ x   ♣ K Q J 10 x

The two hands contain plenty of POWER. Opener's hand is worth about 20 points and responder's about 17. There is, in fact, enough material to produce 15 tricks. But since the opponents can take two aces, the slam is swiftly down. The problem is that both partners are counting extra points for their distribution. That means that there are more than 40 possible points on this deal. It is entirely possible that the partnership could be missing two aces. They must consider CONTROLS as well as power.

THE BLACKWOOD CONVENTION

One way to check up on CONTROLS is a gadget called the BLACKWOOD CONVENTION. A CONVENTION at bridge is a bid that has an ARTIFICIAL MEANING. If we open the bidding with 1 NT, that is a natural bid. It shows a desire to play in notrump. The BLACKWOOD CONVENTION is a bid of 4 NT. It is logical that some unnatural meaning should be assigned to this bid. We would seldom want to bid 4 NT to play that contract, since there is no bonus for bidding 4 NT and making it. So 4 NT is a bid used by many bridge players to find out about controls, specifically, to find out *the number of aces partner holds.*

BLACKWOOD works like this. After you find you have the necessary strength for slam and you agree on a trump suit, a bid of 4 NT says, "Partner, how many aces do you have?" Your partner is obliged to respond to your question according to the following schedule:

With no aces ....he bids 5 ♣
With 1 ....he bids 5 ◇
With 2 ....he bids 5 ♡
With 3 ....he bids 5 ♠
With 4 ....he bids 5 ♣

Note that the response is the same with either no aces or all four aces. Presumably you will be able to tell from your own hand and the previous bidding which holding your partner has.

112

Let's apply the BLACKWOOD CONVENTION and see how it would solve our original problem:

Opener	Responder
1 ♠	2 ♣
3 ♠	4 ♠
4 NT	5 ◇
5 ♠	Pass

Opener feels the values for slam are present, but he stops off to check on controls with BLACKWOOD. When the lack of aces is revealed, the partnership stops just in time. (Whoever uses Blackwood places the contract.) If, however, the two hands were:

Opener	Responder
♠ A Q J 10 x x	♠ K x x
♡ K x	♡ A x x x
◇ K Q J x	◇ x
♣ x	♣ A J x x x

The auction would go like this:

Opener	Responder
1 ♠	2 ♣
3 ♠	4 ♠
4 NT	5 ♡
6 ♠	Pass

Here is another example:

Opener	Responder
♠ A J x x	♠ K Q x x x x
♡ K Q x x	♡ A x
◇ K Q x x	◇ x
♣ x	♣ K x x x

1 ◇	1 ♠
3 ♠	4 NT
5 ◇	5 ♠
Pass	

But . . .	Opener	Responder
	♠ A J x x	♠ K Q x x x x
	♡ K Q x x	♡ A x
	◊ A J x x	◊ x
	♣ x	♣ K x x x
	1 ◊	1 ♠
	3 ♠	4 NT
	5 ♡	6 ♠
	Pass	

We have used a bid of 4 NT in *two ways in this chapter, both as a RAISE OF NOTRUMP, inviting slam; and as the BLACKWOOD CONVENTION, an ace-asking bid.* When you have *balanced* hands, you can bid accurately just on the basis of your point count, so BLACKWOOD is not needed. So a raise of 1 NT to 4 NT is natural — what we call a *quantitative* slam invitation. It is when you are interested in a suit contract, and you may be bidding partly on the basis of good distribution, that you worry about missing aces. That is when you may need to employ BLACKWOOD.

As an extension to the Blackwood Convention, you can continue, after receiving partner's reply to your question about aces, with a bid of 5 NT, which asks him about *KINGS*. His responses are the same as after a 4 NT Blackwood bid, but at the six level.

With no kings . . . . .he bids 6 ♣
With 1 . . . . .he bids 6 ◊
With 2 . . . . .he bids 6 ♡
With 3 . . . . .he bids 6 ♠
With 4 . . . . .he bids 6 ♣

Opener	Responder
♠ A x x	♠ K x
♡ K x x x	♡ A Q J x x
◊ A K x x	◊ Q x x
♣ x x	♣ A K x
1 ◊	2 ♡
3 ♡	4 NT
5 ♡	5 NT
6 ♡	7 ♡

Responder, knowing there is ample power for a slam, uses Blackwood and learns about opener's two aces. He cannot bid a grand slam, however, unless opener also has the two missing kings. If the opponents had either red king, they might well win a trick with it. You must remember one important fact about asking for kings with a bid of 5 NT. *Your side must have all the aces* before you can find out about kings. If you find that an ace is missing, do not ask for kings. Either bid six of your suit or stop at the five level.

As we have seen, whether your side can make a slam may depend on one or more of several factors. Note this well:

THE TIME TO USE THE BLACKWOOD CONVENTION IS WHEN YOU ARE SURE YOUR SIDE HAS ALL THE INGREDIENTS FOR A SLAM CONTRACT — POWER, EVERY SUIT UNDER CONTROL, GOOD TRUMPS — AND THE ONLY REMAINING WORRY IS WHETHER THE OPPONENTS HAVE TWO ACES.

Blackwood, you see, was originally intended *not* as a device to bid slam, but as a way to keep from bidding unmakable slams. The Blackwood Convention will provide you with one, and only one, piece of information — the number of aces your side has. If you can make an intelligent decision about your chances in a slam if you have that one fact, then you use Blackwood.

There are many times, however, when the use of Blackwood is inappropriate:

WHEN NOT TO USE BLACKWOOD

1. DON'T USE BLACKWOOD if you are not sure your side has enough power for slam. Just because you have all the aces, does not mean you have the material for 12 or 13 tricks.
2. DON'T USE BLACKWOOD with a *void* suit in your hand. Blackwood will tell you how many aces your partner holds, but not *which* aces. If you have a void you have to be concerned about *specific* aces, because an ace in your void suit in partner's hand usually would be useless to you.
3. BE CAREFUL ABOUT USING BLACKWOOD if clubs is the agreed suit. Partner's Blackwood response may carry you past five of your suit and too high.
4. DON'T USE BLACKWOOD if you aren't sure your side has every suit under control. A worthless holding, like a small doubleton, in an unbid suit would mean that you might lack a control there.

To repeat, use Blackwood only if you can place the contract accurately if all you need to know is how many aces are held by your side.

INTRODUCTION TO DEFENSIVE PLAY:
PLANNING YOUR STRATEGY

We have looked at some rules the defenders keep in mind as they routinely play to each trick. Some of these rules, like "Second Hand Low," "Third Hand High," and "Cover an Honor with an Honor" are general advice. Others, such as leading the top card of a sequence or playing the cheapest card of equals in third position help the defenders overcome the natural handicap of not being able to see each others' hands.

Now we can start looking at the STRATEGIES the defenders use in situations that require good judgment. It is easy enough to learn which card to lead from a suit, once you have selected a suit. But deciding which suit to lead takes more skill.

STRATEGY AGAINST NOTRUMP CONTRACTS:

The ways declarer has of making tricks — with high cards, intermediates, long cards and so forth — are equally available to the defenders. Therefore the best chance to defeat the contract will usually be to establish long cards and the defense will lead its longest suit at every opportunity. The defenders won't usually change plans in the middle of the hand by switching to some other suit unless there is a compelling reason. The play in notrump is frequently like a race. The declarer is trying to set up his tricks before the defenders can establish enough tricks in a long suit to set him. It is hard to win a race if you must start again half-way through it.

1.
        ♠ K 9 4
        ♡ K Q 10 2
        ◊ 8 4 2
        ♣ Q 9 4

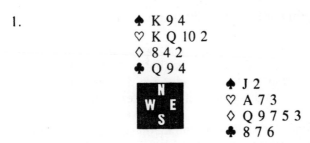

        ♠ J 2
        ♡ A 7 3
        ◊ Q 9 7 5 3
        ♣ 8 7 6

South opened 1 NT and was raised to 3 NT. Your partner leads the ♣ 7 and declarer wins your jack with the ace. Next, he plays the ♡ J. **How should you defend?**

Certainly, you should win your ♡A and *return your last spade,* plugging away at partner's suit hoping to get his long cards established. There are times when you should be reluctant to part with so valuable a card as an ace. But here, there is no point in refusing to take your winner. If you don't win the ace immediately, declarer can continue leading hearts to force your ace. You should, in fact, be anxious to win the trick so that you can lead a spade and set up partner's suit quickly. Here, you should be particularly optimistic about your prospect of tricks in spades. If partner's ♠7 is his fourth-highest card in that suit, he *must* have had Q1087 (and maybe a fifth spade)! The queen, ten and eight are the only spades higher than the seven that we haven't seen.) So one more spade lead will establish partner's suit! Do not consider leading diamonds. RETURN YOUR PARTNER'S LEAD. The complete deal might be:

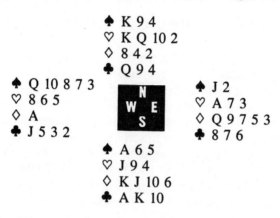

```
                    ♠ K 9 4
                    ♡ K Q 10 2
                    ◊ 8 4 2
                    ♣ Q 9 4
    ♠ Q 10 8 7 3                      ♠ J 2
    ♡ 8 6 5          N                ♡ A 7 3
    ◊ A          W       E            ◊ Q 9 7 5 3
    ♣ J 5 3 2          S              ♣ 8 7 6
                    ♠ A 6 5
                    ♡ J 9 4
                    ◊ K J 10 6
                    ♣ A K 10
```

Note how helpful it was to know that partner's lead was his fourth best.

Another interesting point about this hand: notice that declarer could have won the race by refusing to win the first trick. Now when East wins the ♡A, he cannot return a spade, and declarer has time to set up his ninth trick in diamonds before the defenders' spade suit is established.

While the defenders usually concentrate on setting up their long suit, they may also need to make it tough for declarer to establish *his* tricks. Sometimes, if the defense can prevent declarer from using his best suit, the contract won't have a chance.

2.

♠ 7 5 4
♥ Q 7 5
♦ Q J 10 6 5
♣ 8 2

♠ 8 3 2
♥ K 10 4
♦ A 9 4 2
♣ K 9 6

Declarer, South, opened 2 NT (22-24 high-card points) and was raised to 3 NT. West, your partner, leads the ♠J, showing that his suit is headed by a sequence of cards, of which the jack is the highest. Declarer probably has the ace, king and queen of spades, which means it will be difficult, if not impossible to set up partner's suit. Declarer wins the first trick and leads the ◊K. **How should you defend?**

Your objective should be to keep declarer from using his diamonds by ruining his communication with dummy. So *wait* to win your ◊A until declarer has no more diamonds in his hand. You would *duck* the ◊K. If declarer leads another diamond and partner follows suit, declarer must now be out, so you should win the trick. If partner discards on the second diamond, then declarer had three diamonds to begin with. So you hold up your ace once more.

Suppose you win the second diamond after partner follows twice and return a spade. Declarer wins and leads . . . the ♡J. What do you make of that? **Should you win this trick and return your last spade?**

No, surely not. Declarer has the ♡A, beyond any doubt, and he is tempting you to win this trick so that the ♡Q will be an entry to the good diamonds. It's another time when you can make declarer's job a lot harder by refusing to take a winner. The full deal is:

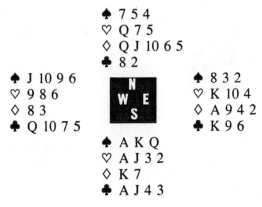

♠ 7 5 4
♥ Q 7 5
♦ Q J 10 6 5
♣ 8 2

♠ J 10 9 6
♥ 9 8 6
♦ 8 3
♣ Q 10 7 5

♠ 8 3 2
♥ K 10 4
♦ A 9 4 2
♣ K 9 6

♠ A K Q
♥ A J 3 2
♦ K 7
♣ A J 4 3

119

If declarer has a trump suit to use, the defenders' approach will be different. For one thing, there is no longer any particular advantage in setting up a long suit, since declarer will use his trumps on the long cards if they are led. Neither can the defense realistically hope to develop any tricks in the trump suit itself, since one of the declarer's main objectives will be to draw outstanding trumps as soon as he can. Against a suit contract, therefore, the defenders must try for tricks with high cards: aces and kings they can take immediately; intermediates that they can establish; and high cards they can win as a result of finesses — finesses that the defense can win or that declarer loses.

DEFENSE AGAINST
SUITS

Take a look at this deal:

3.

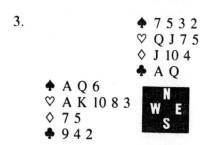

              ♠ 7 5 3 2
              ♥ Q J 7 5
              ♦ J 10 4
              ♣ A Q

♠ A Q 6
♥ A K 10 8 3
♦ 7 5
♣ 9 4 2

South opened 1 ♦ and became declarer at a contract of 4 ♦ . You, West, led your ♥ A. The lead from an ace-king combination, as you have here, is always attractive because you expect to win the first trick and can decide what to lead next after you get a look at what dummy has. **What should you lead at trick two?**

Not your other high heart — that would help declarer by setting up heart tricks in dummy, tricks he may use to discard some of his losers in the black suit. Not your ♠A — you would get one trick that way for sure; but if your *partner* leads a spade, your side would be able to take a winning finesse if declarer had the ♠K, and you would take at least two tricks. The best suit for you to lead here is clubs.

Why clubs? Because, you can tell that if declarer needs to take a finesse in clubs, it will lose. If your partner has the ♣K, it is located favorably for your side, behind dummy's honors. So there may be a potential trick for the defense in clubs.

Declarer plays dummy's queen when you shift to a club, and partner wins the king. Let's move over to his side of the table and see what his problems are:

♠ 7 5 3 2
♡ Q J 7
◊ J 10 4
♣ A

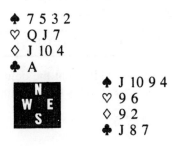

♠ J 10 9 4
♡ 9 6
◊ 9 2
♣ J 8 7

What should he lead?

A club return is pointless. Partner could make his jack high, but dummy could trump it. A heart return might let you score your king, but if declarer has another heart, that is a trick you will always make whether partner leads a heart now or not. Your partner should lead his ♠J.

Why is spades a good suit for him to lead? For the same reason clubs was a good suit for you. Partner can look at dummy, with its worthless spade cards, and figure that any spade finesse declarer tries will lose. Whatever honors you have in spades are located behind declarer's, so there may be tricks for the defenders to take if declarer is forced to finesse.

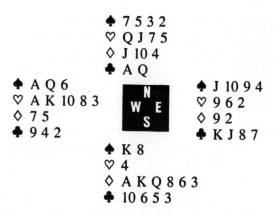

```
          ♠ 7 5 3 2
          ♡ Q J 7 5
          ◇ J 10 4
          ♣ A Q
♠ A Q 6              ♠ J 10 9 4
♡ A K 10 8 3        ♡ 9 6 2
◇ 7 5               ◇ 9 2
♣ 9 4 2             ♣ K J 8 7
          ♠ K 8
          ♡ 4
          ◇ A K Q 8 6 3
          ♣ 10 6 5 3
```

So the best defense here will give the defenders a one-trick set.
This hand illustrates an important strategy on which defenders frequently rely. They tend to LEAD

> **THROUGH STRENGTH AND UP TO WEAKNESS.**

This is just another way of saying that the defenders prefer to lead
suits in which their finesses are likely to work and declarer's are not.

4.

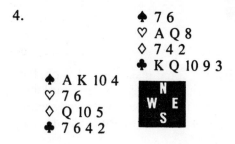

```
             ♠ 7 6
             ♡ A Q 8
             ◇ 7 4 2
             ♣ K Q 10 9 3
♠ A K 10 4
♡ 7 6
◇ Q 10 5
♣ 7 6 4 2
```

Defending against a 4 ♡ contract, you begin by cashing your ♠ A
and ♠ K, dropping declarer's queen and jack. This is not a time to
lead through strength. This time, the dummy strength is *too* impos-
ing. Declarer's plan will be to establish the clubs (if they are not
established already) and use them for tricks, throwing away what
losers he has in diamonds. Here, you must lead a diamond quickly,
hoping you have tricks to take in that suit and they can be collected
before declarer throws his little diamonds away on the clubs.

There is one other simple defensive concept we might mention.
In discussing declarer's play, we have emphasized how he must take
care to do a little planning before he begins to play. The most important part of declarer's planning is a count of his sure tricks. This

is something the defenders can do as well. It takes four tricks to defeat a 4 ♡ contract, and the defense should keep that figure in mind when they are trying to figure out a way to beat such a contract.

5.

♠ A K J 2
♡ 5 4
◊ A 7 4
♣ A Q J 5

♠ 8 7 6
♡ A 9 3
◊ K 10 9 8
♣ K 7 2

North opened 1 ♣, South responded 1 ♠, North raised to 4 ♠. Your partner, West, leads the ♡ Q. This lead indicates that declarer has the ♡ K, so you win the first trick with your ace. **How do you defend from here?**

Are there any more heart tricks for your side? No, declarer will win the next heart, and dummy can trump from then on. Will the defenders win a trick in trumps? No, not a chance. In clubs? Yes, the ♣ K is likely to be worth a trick. What suit will have to produce the other two tricks you need? Diamonds, right? What card *must* partner hold if you are to make two diamond tricks? He'll have to have the ◊ Q, won't he? If declarer has it, behind your king, he will make two tricks in diamonds. So you might as well lead a diamond, hoping for the best.

The full deal:

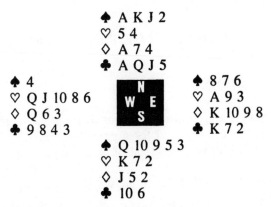

♠ A K J 2
♡ 5 4
◊ A 7 4
♣ A Q J 5

♠ 4
♡ Q J 10 8 6
◊ Q 6 3
♣ 9 8 4 3

♠ 8 7 6
♡ A 9 3
◊ K 10 9 8
♣ K 7 2

♠ Q 10 9 5 3
♡ K 7 2
◊ J 5 2
♣ 10 6

Note that the defenders must lead diamonds *early*, before declarer loses his club finesse and the clubs are set up for diamond discards.

Let's review what we have learned about the DEFENDERS'
STRATEGY:

AGAINST NOTRUMP CONTRACTS:

1. The defense will almost always try to establish long cards
   by leading their longest suit at every opportunity. However . . .
2. The defense may occasionally defer establishing their long
   suit while they try to prevent declarer from making use
   of his best suit. One way the defenders may accomplish
   this is by holding up a high card that declarer must dislodge
   to establish his suit. They may be able to ruin declarer's
   communication.

AGAINST SUIT CONTRACTS:

1. Long cards are of no use to the defense now, since declarer
   can trump them. So the defenders try to win tricks with
   high cards, intermediates they establish, and honors that
   are worth tricks when the defenders take a successful
   finesse or declarer takes one that fails.
2. Hoping to force declarer into taking losing finesses, the
   defenders often adopt the strategy of leading THROUGH
   STRENGTH and UP TO WEAKNESS.
3. The defenders should keep in mind how many tricks they
   must take to defeat the contract and then look for likely
   opportunities to get them.

TEST YOUR COMPREHENSION OF THE MATERIAL IN THIS CHAPTER:

QUIZ ON SLAM BIDDING:

1. How many points are required for a small slam contract?
2. How many points are required for a grand slam contract?
3. Can you add points for your short suits if the hand is to be played
   at notrump?
4. What are some factors that determine whether you can make
   a slam contract?

Partner has opened 1 NT. What do you bid with:

5. ♠ Axx
   ♡ Kxx
   ◊ AQxx
   ♣ KJx

6. ♠ AQx
   ♡ Kxx
   ◊ Kxx
   ♣ KJxx

7. ♠ AQx
   ♡ Kxx
   ◊ AQJxx
   ♣ AJ

8. ♠ —
   ♡ AJ10xxx
   ◊ Kxx
   ♣ AQxx

What would you bid in these situations?

9.
Opener	*Responder*	♠ x
1 ◊	1 ♡	♡ AQxxx
3 ♡	?	◊ Axx
		♣ AJxx

10.
1 ◊	3 ◊	♠ Ax
?		♡ Axx
		◊ AQxxxx
		♣ Kx

11.
1 ♠	3 ♠	♠ AJxxx
?		♡ Kxx
		◊ AJx
		♣ Ax

12.
1 ♡	1 ♠	♠ Axxxx
4 ♣	?	♡ Jx
		◊ Axxx
		♣ Kx

13.
1 ♡	1 ♠	♠ AQxxx
3 ♣	?	♡ xx
		◊ x
		♣ Axxxx

14. 1♣   1♠   ♠ AQxxx
    3♣   ?   ♡ x
                    ◊ AJxx
                    ♣ Qxx

What would you bid in these situations?

15. *Opener*   *Responder*   ♠ KQJxx
    1♠   3♠   ♡ Kx
    ?   ◊ x
                             ♣ AKJxx

16. 1♠   3♠   ♠ KQJxx
    4 NT   5◊   ♡ Kx
    ?   ◊ x
                             ♣ AKJxx

17. 1♠   3♠   ♠ KQJxx
    4 NT   5♠   ♡ Kx
    ?   ◊ x
                             ♣ AKJxx

18. 1♠   3♠   ♠ KQJxx
    4 NT   5♡   ♡ Kx
    ?   ◊ x
                             ♣ AKJxx

19. 1◊   2♠   ♠ AQJxx
    3♠   4 NT   ♡ Kx
    5♡   ?   ◊ Qxx
                             ♣ AKx

You opened 1♣ and partner responded 3♣ (13-15 points, four
or more good clubs, forcing). With which of these hands would
you be willing to use the Blackwood Convention?

20. ♠ —   21. ♠ AKQ   22. ♠ KJxx
    ♡ AKxx   ♡ Kxxx   ♡ Kxxx
    ◊ Kxxx   ◊ A   ◊ x
    ♣ AJxxx   ♣ Jxxxx   ♣ AKQx

23. ♠ xx   24. ♠ AKx
     ♡ AQx   ♡ AQx
     ◊ Axx   ◊ x
     ♣ Axxxx   ♣ KJxxxx

SOLUTIONS:

1. 33
2. 37
3. No
4. Power, every suit under control, good trumps, at least three aces.
5. 6 NT
6. 4 NT, invitational to 6 NT
7. 7 NT
8. 6♡
9. 6♡
10. 6◊
11. 5♠, invitational to slam
12. 6♠
13. 6♣
14. 6♣

In examples 5-14, one player can leap to slam (or invite) based strictly on the POWER he knows the combined hands hold, plus the assurance that every suit must be under control.

15. 4 NT, Blackwood, to check on the possibility of two missing aces.
16. 5♠
17. 7♠
18. 6♠
19. 5 NT, intending to bid a grand slam in spades if partner has the two missing kings.
20. No. DON'T USE BLACKWOOD with a void suit in your hand.
21. No. Your weak trumps are a worry that won't be solved by using Blackwood.
22. No. If partner has only one ace, you will be past 5♣, your only makable game. Be careful about using Blackwood when clubs is the agreed trump.
23. No. This hand is too weak to be interested in a slam.
24. Yes. This hand is fine for Blackwood.

QUIZ ON PLANNING YOUR STRATEGY
AS A DEFENDER:

1.

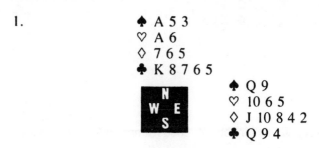

♠ A 5 3
♡ A 6
◊ 7 6 5
♣ K 8 7 6 5

♠ Q 9
♡ 10 6 5
◊ J 10 8 4 2
♣ Q 9 4

South opened 1 NT. North raised to 3 NT. Your partner, West, led the ♠6 and declarer won your queen with the king. He played the ace, king and a low club, giving up a trick to your queen. What should you lead at this point?

2.

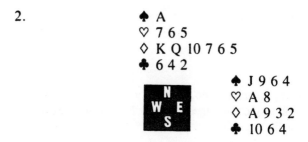

♠ A
♡ 7 6 5
◊ K Q 10 7 6 5
♣ 6 4 2

♠ J 9 6 4
♡ A 8
◊ A 9 3 2
♣ 10 6 4

South opened 1 NT. North raised to 3 NT. Your partner, West, led the ♡2 and you win the ace. What should you lead now?

3.

♠ A 5
♡ 7 5 3
◊ Q J 9 2
♣ Q J 9 8

♠ J 7 3
♡ 9 6 4
◊ 5 4 3
♣ A 7 4 2

South opened 1 NT, North raised to 3 NT. West, your partner, led the ♠6 and dummy's ace won. Declarer now led the ♣8 from dummy. What should you do here?

4.
                    ♠ A J 2
                    ♡ 7 4
                    ◊ J 9 6 4 2
                    ♣ J 10 3
    ♠ 10 9 7
    ♡ A K 10 2
    ◊ 10 3
    ♣ A Q 8 4

South is declarer at a 3 ◊ contract. You cash the ♡A and ♡K, dropping declarer's queen. What should your next lead be?

5.
                    ♠ 7 5
                    ♡ 9 5 3
                    ◊ A Q 10 3
                    ♣ J 9 5 4
                                ♠ A 9 6 4
                                ♡ K 8 2
                       ◊ 6 5 4 2
                                ♣ 8 2

South is declarer at a 3♣ contract. Your partner, West, leads the ♠Q. How should you defend?

6.
                    ♠ K Q J
                    ♡ K 5
                    ◊ A J 4
                    ♣ A K J 9 4
                                ♠ 8 7
                                ♡ A 8 6 4
                    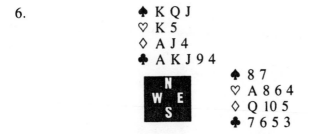   ◊ Q 10 5
                                ♣ 7 6 5 3

North opened 2 NT, South responded 3♠, North raised to 4♠. West, your partner, leads the ♡J, and dummy's king is played. How should you defend?

SOLUTIONS:

1. Lead the ♠9, hoping to establish partner's long suit.
2. This time, partner's lead of the ♡2 suggests that he has only a four-card suit, so there are not enough tricks to establish in that suit. Switch plans and try to keep declarer from using dummy's diamonds. Return a low spade, knocking out dummy's ace, so that declarer cannot use it as an entry after establishing dummy's diamonds. Later, you plan to hold up your ◊A until declarer has no more in his hand, and dummy's suit will be left high and dry.
3. Play the ♣A and lead a spade (partner's suit). You should be delighted to have an opportunity to help establish partner's long suit. (This is a good time to make an exception to the rule "Second Hand Low.")
4. Lead the ♠10. You hope that partner has honors, which will be tricks since they will lie behind dummy's honors. This is a typical THROUGH-STRENGTH situation.
5. Win the ♠A and lead the ♡2 UP TO dummy's WEAKNESS, THROUGH whatever heart STRENGTH declarer may have.
6. Lead the ◊5. You know declarer has the ♡Q, from partner's lead of the jack, so even if partner has the ♠A, you will still need two tricks in diamonds to beat this contract. You must hope partner has the ◊K.

Chapter 8

OPENING BIDS OF MORE THAN ONE OF A SUIT
SCORING

Suppose you are opener with this hand:

(a)
        ♠ A K Q 10 x x
        ♡ A K x
        ◇ x
        ♣ A J 10

If you open just 1♠, the bidding may well die right there! You cannot count on partner to scrape up a response with:

        ♠ x x
        ♡ x x x
        ◇ x x x x
        ♣ Q x x x

even though you could make game in spades. So our bidding structure is incomplete. We need an opening bid to show a hand that will produce a game or slam no matter what responder happens to hold. Hands like the one above are opened with a bid of *TWO* OF A SUIT, 2♠ in this case.

There are two requirements to open the bidding with a strong two-bid. First, you promise that game will be made regardless of partner's holding, so you must furnish sure TRICKS. Note this well: A LARGE NUMBER OF HIGH-CARD POINTS IS NOT NECESSARILY ENOUGH TO FORCE TO GAME.

Look again at the above hand. **How many tricks do you think this hand can reasonably be expected to produce, opposite an unfavorable dummy?** Six tricks in spades, with any luck; two in hearts; at least one in clubs and perhaps two or three if partner has as much as the queen or some length, or if a club is led into your holding. So the certain tricks you need appear to be available.

131

Would you open this hand with two of a suit?

(b)

♠ A K J 10 x
♥ A x
♦ A K Q x x
♣ Q

Yes, you would. You have four or five tricks in spades, one in hearts, four or five in diamonds. You need so little from partner's hand to make game that a 2♠ bid is called for.

The other requirement to open two is excellent DEFENSIVE VALUES. At least 4 Quick Tricks are desired. If you pick up

(c)

♠ K Q J 10 x x x
♥ Q J 10 9
♦ K Q
♣ —

you may well make game in spades opposite little or nothing, but you can't open with a strong two-bid. Your defensive strength is poor, and if the opponents, who may have good distribution and substantial high-card strength, start bidding, you may not defeat them. A strong two-bid promises general strength and the ability to punish the opponents if they climb into the auction. Open 1♠ on this hand. Hands (a) and (b) however, contain the required defensive values to open with a two bid.

AK	= 2 Quick Tricks
AQ	= 1½ Quick Tricks
A	= 1 Quick Trick
KQ	= 1 Quick Trick
K	= ½ Quick Trick

STRONG TWO-BIDS

Opening bids of two of a suit are forcing, and RESPONDER MUST NOT PASS. If your partner opens with two of a suit, he says that game will be made regardless of what you have. You should be happy to hear this even if your hand does not look encouraging. Trust your partner's judgment and keep the bidding alive even if your hand is worthless.

To show WEAKNESS, you respond 2 NT. This warns partner not to count on you for anything. A jump straight to game in partner's suit is (strangely enough) also a weakish response. It shows excellent support for his suit, but nothing else.

Any other response, however, such as a single raise of partner's suit or a new-suit bid, is "positive" and promises some points, at least a trick or two. Such a "positive" response suggests that you would have responded even if the opening bid had been *one* of a suit. When the response is positive, a slam contract is quite possible.

THE REQUIREMENT FOR A "POSITIVE" RESPONSE
STARTS AT ABOUT 7 POINTS.

Suppose your partner has opened 2 ♡. **What do you respond with these hands?**

1. ♠ x x x x
   ♡ x x
   ◇ x x x
   ♣ x x x x

   Bid 2 NT. Don't even consider passing. Partner would be highly irritated. You are forced to respond, trusting partner to have the tricks for game in his own hand.

2. ♠ K x x x x x
   ♡ x x
   ◇ x x x
   ♣ J x

   Respond 2 NT. This warns partner of your weak hand. A 2♠ response would be "positive" and would promise more high-card strength. You plan to show the spades at your next turn.

3. ♠ A Q x x x
   ♡ x x
   ◇ Q x x x
   ♣ x x

   Respond 2♠. This is a minimum positive response.

133

4. ♠ x x   Respond 3 ◊. You will almost surely
   ♡ K x   wind up in a slam. Just think, partner said
   ◊ A J x x x   he could make a game opposite nothing in
   ♣ Q x x x   your hand. However, since your partner-
                   ship is forced to game by partner's strong
opening, you do not need to jump at this stage.

5. ♠ x x   Bid 3 ♡.
   ♡ K x x
   ◊ A J x
   ♣ x x x x x

6. ♠ A K   You could well have a grand slam, but bid
   ♡ K x x   only 3 ♡ to begin with, thereby agreeing
   ◊ Q x x x x   on a trump suit.
   ♣ x x x

7. ♠ x x   Bid 4 ♡, a weakish action showing good
   ♡ Q J x x x   trumps and nothing else.
   ◊ x x x
   ♣ x x x

To summarize:
Opening bids of TWO OF A SUIT are used to show hands with
which opener expects to make game or slam regardless of responder's
holding. The requirements for this action are:

| 1. | Enough certain PLAYING TRICKS in hand to make game. |
| 2. | At least 4 QUICK TRICKS. |

Note that we have not specified a certain number of high-card
points.

Since opener promises enough power to make a game with his
strong two-bid, responder MUST NOT PASS. You must respond,
even with a worthless hand. After an opening two-bid, the auction
must not die until game is reached.

In responding to partner's opening two-bid, your options are:

1. 2 NT, which shows weakness, generally fewer than 7 high-card points.
2. A JUMP TO GAME IN PARTNER'S SUIT, which shows good support for his suit and no outside ace, king, singleton or void.

   Any other response is *positive*, promising at least 7 points and some possible tricks. You would have responded to an opening bid of one, and a slam is possible.

3. A SINGLE RAISE OF PARTNER'S SUIT shows 7+ high-card points and some support for his suit.
4. A NEW-SUIT BID shows 7+ high-card points and a reasonable suit, five or more cards, with some honors.

It might occur to you to wonder why, with hand (c), page 132, you couldn't just open 4♠ and be done with it. There are two answers to this question. First, if you open four and use up a lot of your bidding space, it will be more difficult to determine if your side can make a slam. Second, an opening bid of three of a suit or higher is reserved to show a different kind of hand. It is a bridge paradox that, while opening bids of two of a suit show great strength, openings of three or higher are weak!

In discussing responding to opening bids of one of a suit, we learned that a leap straight to game is a preemptive action, intended to get in the opponents' way and keep them from exchanging information and arriving at an accurate contract. The bidding is often a two-way street. Sometimes you bid to try to find your own best contract; other times, you bid to try to make the opponents' auction less comfortable. This is the idea behind very high opening bids.

Suppose you are the dealer with this hand:

♠ x
♡ K Q J x x x x
◊ x x
♣ J 10 x

135

With this type of hand, you can really get in the opponents' way with relatively little risk. If hearts are trumps, your hand will take a great many trump tricks, so you will not be set severely even in a nine-trick contract. Notice however, that your hand is so weak in defensive strength (you may not take even one trick if some other suit is trumps), that the opponents rate to have the balance of power. They could easily make a game or slam. So you should be interested in preempting and you would open 3♡.

The time to make a preemptive opening is:

---

1. When you have a hand that offers little defense.
2. When you hold a long strong suit that you can rely on for tricks if your suit is trumps.

A preemptive opening is not totally without risk. Notice that you do not really expect to make what you have bid when you open with a preempt. In fact, if you try 3♡ on our example hand and partner has a hand like this:

♠ x x x
♡ x x x
♢ x x x x   (!)
♣ x x x

you will not come anywhere near making your contract. And, don't forget, the opponents may *double* your hopeless contract and increase the size of the penalty you must pay them.

Since the scoring directly affects your strategy when it comes to preemptive openings, perhaps now would be a good time to examine how the game of bridge is scored.

There is more than one method of score-keeping. The traditional way of keeping score is known as RUBBER bridge.

136

OUTLINE FOR SCORING AT RUBBER BRIDGE

TRICK SCORE — what you score for the tricks you bid and make as well as overtricks:

In spades/hearts	30 per trick
In clubs/diamonds	20 per trick
In notrump	40 for the first trick, 30 for every trick thereafter

If the contract is played doubled and made, multiply the usual trick score by two. If it is played doubled and redoubled and made, multiply the usual trick score by four.

To score game, you need 100 or more points in trick scores "below the line."

BONUSES —

Rubber bonus	500 if you win two games out of three 700 if you win two games and the opponents do not win a game
Slam bonuses	500 for a small slam not vulnerable 750 for a small slam vulnerable* 1000 for a grand slam not vulnerable 1500 for a grand slam vulnerable
Honors	100 for four trump honors in one hand 150 for all five trump honors in one hand 150 for all four aces in one hand at notrump. (The honor bonuses may be claimed by a defender.)
For making a doubled or redoubled contract	50
For doubled and redoubled overtricks	100 per trick doubled, not vulnerable 200 per trick doubled, vulnerable 200 per trick redoubled, not vulnerable 400 per trick redoubled, vulnerable

*Vulnerable means your side has won a game (see page 139).

PENALTIES — what you score if you set the opponents' contract:

> 50 per trick, undoubled, not vulnerable
> 100 per trick, undoubled, vulnerable
> 100 for first trick . . .
> 200 for every trick thereafter, doubled, not vulnerable
> 200 for first trick . . .
> 300 for every trick thereafter, doubled, vulnerable.

If redoubled, multiply the doubled penalty by two.

The objective in RUBBER bridge scoring is to win the RUBBER, which consists of the best two-out-of-three games. Two or more part-score contracts may accumulate toward the making of game. You don't have to make a game all on one hand. As you can see, your side scores more points if you win the rubber by making two games before the opponents make a game.

Each individual rubber is scored on a diagram that looks like this:

WE | *THEY*

Note the horizontal line in the middle of the diagram. All points that count toward scoring game, that is, the points you score for bidding and making contracts, go "BELOW THE LINE." Everything else — bonuses, penalties, points scored for overtricks, go "ABOVE THE LINE."

The number of points awarded for various contracts, bonuses, and penalties is shown in our outline. Let's look at a sample rubber and see what the scoring diagram above would look like as the rubber proceeded.

WE | *THEY*

30
90

HAND 1: Our side (WE") play 3♠ and make four. We score 90 points "below the line." These are the only points that count toward fulfilling game, since we bid only as high as three. The other 30 points, for the overtrick that was made, goes "above the line." Our side, it is said, now has 90 partscore, or a "90 leg."

138

WE	THEY
40	
30	
90	
20	

HAND 2: WE play 1♣ and make three. WE score 20 points below the line, 40 above the line. Since scoring game required 100 points in trick scores below the line, and WE now have more than that, WE score game, the first one of this rubber. If you look at the trick scores that are awarded for contracts in the various suits and in notrump, and you will see why 3 NT, 4♡, 4♠, 5♣ and 5 ◊ are game contracts. Both sides must now start over toward making a second game.

There is a new and important consideration to remember at this point in the rubber. Now that our side has made one of the two games we need to win the rubber, WE are said to be "VULNERABLE." This is a good-news bad-news situation. The good news is that, when you become vulnerable, you need win only one more game to capture the rubber, and the substantial bonus that goes along with it. The bad news is that if you fail to make a contract you bid when vulnerable, the penalties are increased. So when you are vulnerable, you must combine boldness with discretion.

WE	THEY
300	
40	
30	
90	
20	

HAND 3: THEY play 4♠ doubled, down two. WE score 300 points in penalties for setting the opponents two tricks, not vulnerable. These points, remember, go above the line.

WE	THEY
300	
40	
30	
90	
20	
60	

HAND 4: WE play 2 ♡, making two. WE score 60 points below the line, and have another "leg."

WE	THEY
300	30
40	100
30	500
90	
20	
60	180

HAND 5: A disaster. THEY play 6 ♠ and make seven. Also, declarer holds four of the five trump honors. THEY score 180 points below the line, 30 above the line for the overtrick. In addition, there are bonuses: THEY score 500 points for the small slam, not vulnerable; and 100 for the honors. THEY are now VULNERABLE as well, and the fact that THEY have made a game wipes out the 60 partscore that WE had. Both sides now start fresh toward the third game in the rubber. WE get to keep our 60 points, even though it no longer counts toward scoring a game.

WE	THEY
	800
300	30
40	100
30	500
90	
20	
60	180

HAND 6: WE play 3 NT doubled, down three. THEY score 800 points in penalties. Since WE are vulnerable, the penalty is 200 points for the first undertrick, 300 for every one after that.

WE	THEY
500	
50	
400	800
300	30
40	100
30	500
90	
20	
60	180
480	

HAND 7: WE play 4♡ doubled and redoubled, making five. This may take a little while to add up. WE score 480 points below the line for the tricks. Since the contract was played doubled and redoubled, the usual trick score is multiplied by four. The redoubled overtrick, vulnerable, is worth another 400. There is a 50 point bonus for making a doubled contract. And to top it all off, we have scored game and won the rubber, picking up a 500 point bonus for that.

The next step is to total the scores for this rubber. WE have scored 1970 points, THEY have scored 1610 points. So WE won the rubber by 360 points (often rounded off to the nearest 100; you would say, "WE won a four") . . . Now you can begin a new rubber.

Now we can return to our discussion of preemptive opening bids, and see how the scoring makes preemption such a sound tactic to employ. Look at this hand again, the one on which we recommended a 3♡ opening:

♠ x
♡ K Q J x x x x
◊ x x
♣ J 10 x

This hand will probably take six tricks if hearts are trumps, even if partner has nothing. So if you were to open 3♡, not vulnerable, get doubled, and find a worthless dummy, you would have to concede the opponents 500 points for the three-trick set. But if the dummy does look like this:

♠ x x x
♡ x x x
◊ x x x x
♣ x x x

what do you think the opponents could make if you left them room in the bidding to investigate carefully for their best contract? They could make a grand slam, couldn't they? And they would score a great many more than 500 points. If they were vulnerable, it would be even worse to allow them to buy the contract, for they would win the rubber bonus as well! Very expensive for your side.

Now suppose the opponents are not vulnerable and your side is. This is not a good time for you to offer the opponents a penalty in exchange for what they could score by bidding. There is no rubber bonus for them to score, and the penalties they will earn for setting you are greater. So they will be more inclined to double you and take what they can get.

The best time to preempt is when you are not vulnerable and the opponents are.

Of course, it is not a certainty that you will go down when you open with a preempt. If your partner happens to have a good hand, you will make your contract. Perhaps he will even have enough for you to make game.

In responding to a preemptive opening by your partner, keep in mind that he will have six or seven sure tricks as well as an excellent suit that almost surely will be your side's best one. If you have four sure tricks in your hand (aces and kings are best), raise him to game in his suit. You do *not* need any particular support for partner's suit, since it will be strong enough to stand on its own.

Suppose you are dealer with the following hands, neither side vulnerable. What would your action be on each one?

1. ♠ x   Open 3♡.
    ♡ K Q 10 x x x x
    ◊ Q x x
    ♣ x x

2. ♠ x x   Pass. You might lose several tricks in
    ♡ Q x x x x x x   hearts with this hand, so a preempt could
    ◊ Q J x   be too expensive if the opponents doubled.
    ♣ x

3. ♠ A J x   Open 1♡. Remember that a preemptive
    ♡ K Q J x x x x   bid is made with weakness. This is a
    ◊ Q x   normal opening bid.
    ♣ x

142

4. ♠ x   Open 4♥. This time you have an extra
   ♥ K Q J x x x x x   winner in your suit, so you can make the
   ♦ J 10 x   opponents start looking for their best con-
   ♣ x   tract at an even higher level.

5. ♠ —   Open 5♣! You might drive the opponents
   ♥ Q x x   crazy.
   ♦ x
   ♣ K Q J x x x x x x

To summarize:
Opening bids of THREE OR MORE are preemptive, designed to
crowd the bidding and prevent the opponents from exchanging information and bidding accurately. Preemptive openings are good tac-
tics when you have the right kind of hand to use them. The best time
to preempt is:

```
1.  When you have a hand that offers little defense.
2.  When you hold a long, strong suit (typically, seven cards
    when you preempt at the three level, eight or nine cards
    if you preempt at an even higher level) which you can re-
    ly on for tricks, but only if your suit is trumps.
3.  When the vulnerability is in your favor (you are not
    vulnerable, they are.).
```

When your partner opens with a preemptive bid below game, you
can count on him for six or seven sure tricks. With four sure tricks
in your own hand, therefore raise him to game.

INTRODUCTION TO DEFENSIVE PLAY:

(Before studying this section, review the introductory material on
opening leads in Chapter 3.)

CHOOSING A SUIT TO LEAD;
CHOOSING AN OPENING LEAD

If you have to lead to a trick, there are two problems. First, you
must pick a suit; then you must decide which card to lead from the
suit. In a previous chapter, we learned the importance of leading the
right card from your suit. Now we will look at some factors that
influence your choice of which suit to lead

AGAINST NOTRUMP CONTRACTS:

As we have seen, the defenders' best hope of tricks against a notrump contract is likely to be their long cards. So in this case you will almost always begin by leading your longest suit. With two suits of equal length, lead the stronger suit. Continue leading your longest suit at every opportunity, hoping to get your length established. Don't switch to some other suit unless there is a compelling reason.

It is really more accurate to say that the suit you lead is a suit in which your *partnership* has length. If your partner has bid, especially if he has opened the bidding in a major suit or overcalled (in any suit), he is likely to have a good suit. You should lead his bid suit unless you have a very strong suit of your own and an entry to cash your long cards. (We will discuss Overcalls in detail on page 155.)

If your hand is very weak, you may decide to speculate on where partner has length and lead that suit, even if your partner has not bid.

AGAINST SUIT CONTRACTS:

The element of a trump suit introduces new problems. There is no particular advantage to establishing long cards now, since declarer will be able to use his trumps to ruff.

In general, several holdings offer an attractive lead:

1. As we have seen, suits that contain sequential holdings, like KQJx or QJ10x make excellent leads. The lead of the king from KQJx is most unlikely to cost you anything — if declarer has the ace, that is a trick you cannot deny him — but you will establish some intermediates for tricks. Almost as good is a holding such as KQx or QJx. Perhaps partner will hold some high card that will give your holding a boost.

2. Even though establishing long cards is not really productive, leading a long suit is still worth consideration, even against a suit contract. Perhaps declarer will be correspondingly short in this suit, in which case your lead may be of no help to him in establishing tricks.

3. A suit in which you have a worthless holding might make a good lead. Perhaps your partner holds some of the missing honors and you can establish or cash some tricks in *his* hand. It may, however, be dangerous to lead away from a suit that contains one solitary honor (like Kxxxx or Qxxx). You may let declarer make a trick with one of his lesser intermediate cards.

4. A singleton can be a devastating lead. Perhaps partner will produce the ace and return the suit for you to trump. You may accomplish the same thing by leading a doubleton, but your chances of trumping are obviously not as good.
5. If nothing in particular appeals to you, you might:
   (a) lead trumps. If nothing else, you probably won't give declarer any tricks that aren't always his anyway.
   (b) lay down an unsupported ace.
   (c) gamble with a lead like the queen from Qx, hoping to find something really good in partner's hand.
   (d) lead a suit the opponents have not bid, regardless of your holding.
   (e) lead through the strength of dummy's first-bid suit.

YOUR STRATEGY OF CHOOSING A SUIT TO LEAD IS USUALLY INFLUENCED BY THE DICTUM OF LEADING THROUGH STRENGTH AND UP TO WEAKNESS. ALWAYS TAKE THE STRENGTHS AND WEAKNESSES OF DUMMY INTO ACCOUNT WHEN YOU ARE SELECTING A LEAD.

OPENING LEADS:

If your right-hand opponent is declarer, you must lead to the first trick (making the OPENING LEAD) *before* you see dummy. That is why opening leads are one of the toughest parts of bridge.

Any of the suggested leads listed above might make a reasonable opening lead, particularly the lead from a good sequence. The lead from a suit headed by an ace-king is perhaps the best sequential lead of all — you can expect to win the first trick, and you may be able to better judge what to lead next after you see the dummy.

Of course, if partner has bid, the lead of his bid suit is always worth considering. If your partner has overcalled suggesting a very good suit, you should almost always lead his suit. If he has opened the bidding, you should lead his suit unless you hold a very attractive lead, such as a singleton, an ace-king combination or an excellent sequence. If partner responds to your opening in a suit, remember that he promises no special suit quality. That means the lead of his suit in this case is not guaranteed to be productive.

TEST YOUR COMPREHENSION OF THE MATERIAL IN THIS CHAPTER:

QUIZ ON OPENING BIDS OF MORE THAN ONE:

I. You are the dealer, with neither side vulnerable. What is your action with each of these hands?

1. ♠ AKx	2. ♠ AJx	3. ♠ AKQxxx
♡ Ax	♡ Axx	♡ Axx
◊ AKxxxxx	◊ AKxx	◊ Kxx
♣ x	♣ KQx	♣ x

4. ♠ AKQxx	5. ♠ AJx	6. ♠ —
♡ AKQxx	♡ KQx	♡ xxx
◊ —	◊ AKxxx	◊ xx
♣ Qxx	♣ KQ	♣ KQJxxxxx

7. ♠ Axxxxxx	8. ♠ QJ10xxxx	9. ♠ AQJxxxx
♡ Qx	♡ x	♡ Qx
◊ xx	◊ Kxxx	◊ KJx
♣ xx	♣ x	♣ x

10. ♠ x	11. ♠ KJxxxx	12. ♠ KQJxxxxx
♡ xxx	♡ Qx	♡ —
◊ AK	◊ Kx	◊ xxx
♣ Jxxxxx	♣ Qx	♣ Qx

13. ♠ AQxx	14. ♠ x	15. ♠ AKQxxx
♡ xx	♡ xx	♡ AKxx
◊ AKQ	◊ AQJxxxx	◊ —
♣ Axxx	♣ Qxx	♣ KQx

II. Partner opens 2♡ and your right-hand opponent passes. What is your response with each of these hands?

1. ♠ xxxx	2. ♠ KJxxx	3. ♠ Qxxx
♡ x	♡ xx	♡ Jx
◊ xxxx	◊ xxx	◊ Qxx
♣ xxxx	♣ xxx	♣ Jxxx

4. ♠ Ax	5. ♠ AK	6. ♠ xx
♡ KJx	♡ KJx	♡ QJxxx
◊ xxxx	◊ Jxxxx	◊ xxxx
♣ xxxx	♣ xxx	♣ xx

7. ♠ xx	8. ♠ KQJxx	9. ♠ Axx
♡ Jxx	♡ xx	♡ x
◊ Kxxx	◊ Kxx	◊ AJxxx
♣ xxxx	♣ xxx	♣ xxxx

III. Partner opens 3♠ and your right-hand opponent passes. What action do you take with each of these hands?

1. ♠ x	2. ♠ xxx	3. ♠ Axx
♡ AKxx	♡ Kxx	♡ QJxx
◊ Axxx	◊ Axxx	◊ KJx
♣ AJxx	♣ QJx	♣ AKx

SOLUTIONS:

I. 1. 2◊   9. 1♠
    2. 1◊   10. Pass
    3. 1♠   11. Pass
    4. 2♠   12. 4♠
    5. 2 NT   13. 1♣
    6. 4♣   14. 3◊
    7. Pass   15. 2♠
    8. 3♠

II. 1. 2 NT. You must respond.
     2. 2 NT. Too weak to bid 2♠.
     3. 2 NT
     4. 3♡
     5. 3♡.   Slam is almost certain.
     6. 4♡,   showing good support and nothing else.
     7. 2 NT, planning to raise hearts next.
     8. 2♠
     9. 3◊

III. 1. 4♠.   You have the tricks to raise. Support for part-
               ner's suit is not needed.
     2. Pass
     3. 3 NT. You hope to run partner's spade suit. You
               might be off four fast tricks in a 4♠ contract.

147

QUIZ ON RUBBER BRIDGE SCORING:

I. You are the scorekeeper. Keep a score diagram for the following imaginary rubber.

HAND 1: WE play 4♠ and make five.
HAND 2: THEY play 2♣ and make four, with a hundred honors.
HAND 3: THEY play 3◊ doubled, down one.
HAND 4: WE play 3 NT, down two.
HAND 5: THEY play 1♠ and make three.
HAND 6: WE play 4♠ doubled and redoubled, down two.
HAND 7: WE play 3♡ doubled, making four.

II. You are the scorekeeper. Keep a scoring diagram for the following imaginary rubber.

HAND 1: WE play 3♡, making five.
HAND 2: THEY play 3 NT, making four.
HAND 3: WE play 4♠ doubled, down three, with a hundred and fifty honors.
HAND 4: THEY play 2◊, making three.
HAND 5: WE play 6♠, making six.
HAND 6: WE play 5♣ doubled, down one.
HAND 7: THEY play 7◊, making seven.

III. Answer the following questions. Try not to refer to the scoring outline.

1. How many points do diamonds score per trick bid and made?
2. How many points are needed to score a game?
3. How many points does notrump score per trick bid and made?
4. What is the rubber bonus for winning two games in a row?
5. What is the bonus for a small slam, vulnerable?
6. How many points are scored for four trump honors in one hand?
7. What do you score for making a doubled contract?
8. What is the penalty for a one-trick set, undoubled, not vulnerable?
9. What is the penalty for a three-trick set, undoubled, vulnerable?
10. What is the penalty for a four-trick set, doubled, not vulnerable?

SOLUTIONS:

I.

WE	THEY
700	1000
50	60
200	200
100	100
30	40
120	
180	40
	30
1380	1470

THEY win the rubber by 90 points, usually rounded off to the nearest hundred. You would say, "THEY won a one."

II.

WE	THEY
	1500
	500
	200
500	20
150	500
60	30
90	100
180	40
	140
980	3030

THEY "won a twenty-one."

III.   1. 20
      2. 100
      3. 40 for the first trick, 30 for every subsequent trick.
      4. 700
      5. 750
      6. 100
      7. 50, plus the usual trick score is doubled, plus whatever bonuses may apply.
      8. 50
      9. 300
     10. 700

QUIZ ON OPENING LEADS:

I. The opponents have bid 1 NT - 3 NT, and you must make the opening lead. What card would you choose from each of these hands?

1. ♠ K J 8 6 3   2. ♠ K J 6 2   3. ♠ 7 5
   ♡ A 5 4   ♡ A 8   ♡ A 9 7 5 2
   ◊ 6 4   ◊ K 10 8 6 3   ◊ 8 7 4
   ♣ 10 5 3   ♣ 6 5   ♣ A K 4

4. ♠ 7 6 3   5. ♠ Q J 10 5
   ♡ J 10   ♡ 8 4
   ◊ J 9 7 6 2   ◊ 8 7 3
   ♣ 8 7 4   ♣ K 9 8 3

II. The auction has gone:

(Left Hand Opponent)		(Right Hand Opponent)	
LHO	Partner	RHO	You
1♣	1♡	1♠	Pass
2♣	Pass	3 NT	Pass
Pass	Pass		

You must make the opening lead. What card would you choose from each of these hands?

1. ♠ 8 6 3   2. ♠ K J 9 7 3   3. ♠ 8 7 3 2
   ♡ J 6   ♡ Q 7   ♡ 8
   ◊ 8 7 6   ◊ 8 5   ◊ A J 9 6 4
   ♣ J 9 6 4 2   ♣ 9 7 6 3   ♣ 8 7 6

4. ♠ A 8 6 2   5. ♠ 8 6 5 3
   ♡ Q 9 2   ♡ 10 3
   ◊ 8 6   ◊ A 9 7 5 4 2
   ♣ 9 7 6 2   ♣ 8

III. The opponents have bid 1♡ - 3♡ - 4♡. You must make the opening lead. What card would you choose from each of these hands?

1. ♠ A K 7   2. ♠ K Q 10 4   3. ♠ 9 8 6 4
   ♡ 7 6   ♡ 8 7 5   ♡ A 8 6
   ◊ Q 9 7 3   ◊ J 9 5 3   ◊ 5
   ♣ 10 8 6 3   ♣ A 7   ♣ Q 8 7 6 2

4. ♠ K 7 6   5. ♠ Q 10 4 2
   ♡ 6 5   ♡ 8 7 5
   ◊ K 7 6   ◊ K 9 6
   ♣ 9 7 6 5 2   ♣ A 8 6

IV. Partner opened 1♠, right-hand opponent overcalled 2♡, left-hand opponent raised to 4♡, passed out. What opening lead would you choose from each of these hands?

1. ♠ Q 5   2. ♠ Q 8 6 4   3. ♠ J 8
   ♡ 7 6 3   ♡ 8 7 4   ♡ 7 6 5
   ◊ J 10 9 4   ◊ 4   ◊ A K 4
   ♣ 6 5 4 3   ♣ 10 8 6 5 2   ♣ 9 7 6 5 2

4. ♠ 10 6 4   5. ♠ 6 4 2
   ♡ 8 7   ♡ 7 5
   ◊ K 10 8 6   ◊ Q J 10 8
   ♣ Q 10 8 7   ♣ K 9 7 5

V The auction has gone:

LHO	Partner	RHO	You
1♣	1♠	2♣	Pass
2 NT	Pass	3♡	Pass
4♡	Pass	Pass	Pass

You must make the opening lead against this contract. What card would you choose from each of these hands?

1. ♠ J 8
   ♡ 7 6 5
   ◊ Q J 10 9 4
   ♣ 8 7 4

2. ♠ A 7
   ♡ 8 7 6
   ◊ 10 9 8 6 4
   ♣ K 7 4

3. ♠ Q 9 2
   ♡ 9 8 6
   ◊ A 8 7 5
   ♣ 7 6 5

4. ♠ Q 5
   ♡ 9 8 6 3
   ◊ A K 5
   ♣ 9 7 6 3

5. ♠ J 8 6
   ♡ 7 6
   ◊ 8 7 5 3
   ♣ A 8 6 5

VI The auction has gone:

LHO	Partner	RHO	You
1◊	Pass	1♠	Pass
2♠	Pass	4♠	Pass
Pass	Pass		

You must make the opening lead. What card would you choose from each of these hands?

1. ♠ 6 4
   ♡ K Q J 8
   ◊ A 7 4
   ♣ J 9 7 5

2. ♠ Q 7 5
   ♡ K 7 6 3
   ◊ 9 8 7
   ♣ K 8 6

3. ♠ A 7 5
   ♡ 5
   ◊ J 8 6 4
   ♣ J 8 7 6 3

4. ♠ A 8 6
   ♡ 8 6
   ◊ A 8 7 5
   ♣ J 10 9 4

5. ♠ A 6
   ♡ J 9 7 6 4
   ◊ K 10 4 2
   ♣ Q 7

SOLUTIONS:

I. 1. ♠6.
    2. ◊6; lead your **longest** suit, even though your spades are stronger.
    3. ♡5; do not cash your high clubs; you may need them as **entries** to lead your long suit again.
    4. ♡J; your hand is so weak, without a single entry, that you should try to find partner's long suit.
    5. ♠Q.

II. 1. ♡J.
    2. ♡Q. Do not lead your own suit when partner has suggested a good suit with his overcall. Also, your right-hand opponent showed length in spades
    3. ◊6, with only a singleton in partner's suit. Note you need only a little help to establish your suit.
    4. ♡2.
    5. ♡10. The quality of your diamond suit is too poor to consider leading.

III 1. ♠A.
    2. ♠K.
    3. ◊5. Perhaps partner has the Ace and will win and return the suit for you to trump.
    4. ♣5. The lead of a worthless suit can be effective, since you might be leading to some honors in partner's hand. You might help declarer if you lead from either of your kings.
    5. ♡5. Lead a trump, for safety, since you have no attractive lead in any other suit.

IV. 1. ♠Q.
 2. ◊4; partner has a good hand for his opening; perhaps he has the ◊A (or ♡A!).
 3. ◊A.
 4. ♡7. Sometimes a trump is a good lead because it is relatively safe, unlikely to give away a trick. Often a trump lead by the defense will hurt declarer's cause by preventing him from making extra tricks by using his trumps separately. You draw two of declarer's trumps with your lead. Here, partner has the spades and you have tricks in the minor suits. So declarer mostly likely will have to try for his contract by making extra trump tricks.
 5. ◊Q.

V. 1. ♠J; almost always lead partner's suit when he overcalls.
 2. ♠A.
 3. ♠2.
 4. ◊A, although the ♠Q is a close second choice.
 5. ♣A. This is a rare exception. You plan to lead another club after taking your Ace, expecting partner to trump! The opponents bid and raised clubs before they settled into hearts, so partner should have one club at most.

VI. 1. ♡K.
 2. ◊9. No other lead is particularly attractive. A diamond lead looks safe.
 3. ♡5; hoping to trump further heart leads.
 4. ♣J.
 5. ♡6. The lead of your longest suit here looks safest. Declarer probably is short in this suit, so your lead will be of no help to him.

Chapter 9

WHEN THE OPPONENTS OPEN THE BIDDING

We have examined the system that most players use in constructive bidding. Of course, at times the *opponents* will have most of the strength and your side will not bid at all. You will have to hope that your opposition is not as skillful as you at bidding precisely. You cannot bid without high cards or any other source of tricks — remember that the opponents can double you and inflict a severe penalty.

Quite often, *both* sides may have a good trump suit and a share of the high-card strength, and the bidding will be *competitive*. A knowledge of constructive bidding (when you and your partner have things all to yourself) is only one part of the good bidder's skills. You must also know something about bidding in competition and judging competitive auctions. Fine judgment in competitive situations can be acquired only after you have played for a while. But we can start learning some basic ideas to keep in mind when the auction turns competitive.

Let's look at OVERCALLS, one of the most important situations in competitive bidding. Suppose your right-hand opponent has opened the bidding. You are next to call and must decide whether to get into this auction.

Even though the other side has made the first bid, there are still plenty of reasons why you might like to bid:

1. A game contract for your side is still possible.
2. Perhaps you can arrive in a good partscore contract.
3. You might find a profitable sacrifice against the opponents' contract.
4. Your competition may push the opponents up to a level where you can set them.
5. Your interference could cause the opponents to bid less accurately.
6. You can tell partner what to lead against the opponents' contract.

Unfortunately, there are also some dangers involved in getting into the opponents' auction. The main one is:

> YOU MAY BE DOUBLED AND SET BADLY.

When you overcall you are really sticking your neck out. Your right-hand opponent has opened the bidding and has at least 13 points, quite possibly more. Your left-hand opponent's hand is a complete mystery.

♠ A 6 4
♡ Q 8 5
◊ K 9 2
♣ A 7 5 3

If you are dealer, you open 1 ♣. This is dangerous, in a way, but making the first bid in the auction offers you some safety. If you pass hands like this, you will miss many games and partscores.

Now suppose your right-hand opponent opens 1 ♡. Things have changed. It is too dangerous for you to do anything but PASS. To overcall 2 ♣ would really be sticking your neck out. Suppose your left-hand opponent has some points (if he has only 8 he knows that his side has more than yours), and some clubs (so that he knows you don't have a good suit to make up for what you lack in high cards). He could double, knowing you cannot possibly make your eight-trick contract. Sadly, it is just when you are doubled and need help in dummy that partner is likely to put down a collection of nothing. You could easily be defeated four or five tricks.

Balanced hands are defensive hands. You have prospects of four tricks if you wind up defending an opposing contract, but only the same four if you are declarer. So it is best to not bid, in spite of your 13 points. YOU DO NOT HAVE TO ACT WITH 13 POINTS, OR EVEN MORE, IF AN OPPONENT OPENS THE BIDDING IN FRONT OF YOU. Your best chance to score points on this hand will probably be to set an opposing contract. You have too many losing cards in your hand to want to be declarer.

Note this well:

> SINCE IT IS DANGEROUS TO BID WHEN THE OPPONENTS HAVE STARTED THE AUCTION, OVERCALLS ARE BASED ON A GOOD SUIT. POSSESSION OF GOOD TRUMPS WILL MAKE IT HARDER FOR THE OPPONENTS TO DOUBLE YOU AND PENALIZE YOU HEAVILY.

The sure tricks that a good trump suit can provide give you a security blanket when you enter the opponents' auction. If you decide to get into the auction, there are several ways to do it, and almost all of them provide you with the safety of a good trump suit. Let's take a look at your options. Right-hand opponent deals and opens 1 ♡ with neither side vulnerable:

YOU CAN STILL HAVE A HAPPY RESULT EVEN THOUGH THE OPPONENTS BID FIRST.

1. ♠ A K J 9 x   This is a minimum 1♠ OVERCALL.
   ♡ x x   Note that you have a good suit, the pri-
   ◊ K x x x   primary requirement of an OVERCALL.
   ♣ x x   Most players prefer to have a good hand
                       as well, at least an opening bid.

2. ♠ A x   This time you would have to OVER-
   ♡ x x x   CALL at the two-level on a broken suit.
   ◊ K J x x x   If left-hand opponent has a few points and
   ♣ K x x   some of your diamonds, he could double
                       and set you several tricks. It is too
                       dangerous to bid. Pass.

3. ♠ J x   This is what a two-level OVERCALL
   ♡ x x   should look like — a good suit and a sound
   ◊ A Q 10 x x x   hand. (You might have more than this, but
   ♣ K Q x   you won't have any less.) Bid 2 ◊.

4. ♠ K Q J 9 x x x   You would have opened this hand 3♠,
   ♡ x   a PREEMPTIVE action, and the same bid
   ◊ x x x   may still be effective in causing the
   ♣ J x   opponents to bid less accurately. (Be
                       careful if vulnerable, however.)

5. ♠ K Q J 9 x x   This is a hand with which you would like
   ♡ x   to PREEMPT, but it is too dangerous to
   ◊ x x x   jump to 3♠. You have fewer winners
   ♣ J x x   than in the previous example, and if you
                       were doubled, the penalty might be

greater than you could afford. You can, however, bid 2♠. JUMP
OVERCALLS are played as "mini-preempts." They show a good
suit, usually six cards, but a poor hand.

6. ♠ K x x x   This is a desirable hand to get into the bid-
   ♡ x   ding with, because if partner has support
   ◊ A J x x   for any of your suits, you will provide a
   ♣ K Q x x   lot of tricks. But if you must choose a suit
                       to bid, you have no guarantee that partner

will have support for the one you choose. What you would like to
do here is overcall in your partner's best suit! Wouldn't it be nice
if you could look into partner's hand and see where he has length?
Well, surprisingly enough, there is way to do exactly that.

Back in the early days of bridge, people noticed that if someone opened the bidding one of a suit, the next player was very unlikely to have the right kind of hand for a penalty double. If the opening bid were, say, 1 ♡, you were almost never dealt a hand with enough points and enough good hearts that you could expect to punish the opponents severely in their one-level contract. So, a more practical meaning was assigned to a DOUBLE OF THE OPPONENTS' OPENING OF ONE OF A SUIT. When your right-hand opponent opens 1 ♡ and you double

East	*South*
1 ♡	Double

your double is not for penalties, but for TAKEOUT. The double means that you have a good hand and a desire to compete. North is not supposed to pass, but to TAKE THE DOUBLE OUT, most frequently to HIS BEST SUIT. This is how your partnership can arrive in your best trump suit when SOUTH HAS A GOOD HAND BUT NO PARTICULARLY GOOD SUIT.

A TAKEOUT DOUBLE (made by simply saying "Double") can be made on one of two types of hands. You might have a hand like #6, with at least an opening bid plus support for all the unbid suits.

You will also start with a TAKEOUT DOUBLE if you have a very strong hand and a good suit of your own.

7. ♠ A K J x x   You could OVERCALL 1 ♠ with this
    ♡ x x   hand, but partner might not think you had
    ◊ A Q x   so many points. The way to handle this
    ♣ A x x   kind of hand is to DOUBLE at your first
                   turn. Partner will respond, and you then
show your spades. This sequence, DOUBLE-then-bid, shows a powerful hand, 18 points or more, and a good suit.

Later we will discuss how your partner responds to your takeout double. Meanwhile, there are a few other possible actions to consider:

8. ♠ 10 x x   OVERCALL 1 NT. This shows the same
    ♡ K Q x   kind of hand as a notrump opening. But
    ◊ A K J x   to overcall 1 NT, you need some high
    ♣ A x x   cards in the opponent's suit. If the open-
                              ing bid were 1 ♠, you could not overcall
1 NT. The opponents might take too many spade tricks against that
contract. Over 1 ♠, you would make a TAKEOUT DOUBLE, asking partner to bid a suit.

9. ♠ x x   The best action with this hand is to PASS.
    ♡ K Q J x x   Remember, you cannot double, since that
    ◊ A x x   would be for takeout and your partner
    ♣ K J x   would bid, expecting you to have support
                              for the unbid suits. If you pass, perhaps
they will bid further and go down.

10. ♠ A K Q 10 x x   You would have opened 2 ♠ as dealer,
    ♡ —   showing a game-forcing hand. That bid
    ◊ A x x x   is unavailable now. Remember that if you
    ♣ A K x   OVERCALL 2 ♠, you show a "mini-
                              preempt." A 4 ♠ overcall is also unsuit-
able, even though you can expect to make the contract. Partner would
think you had a preemptive-type hand, maybe with eight good spades
and nothing else.

    There is a special bid to handle a hand like this. A bid of the op-
ponents' suit here is used to say, "Partner, don't be intimidated by
their opening bid. I would have opened with a forcing two-bid, and
we have a game." Your overcall in the opponent's suit is called a
CUEBID and is absolutely forcing on partner, just as an opening
two-bid by you would be forcing. Partner must not leave you in 2 ♡.
He bids 2 NT to show a very bad hand, just as he would respond
2 NT to an opening two-bid to show weakness. You can bid 4 ♠
at your next turn. This way you tell partner that you have a lot of
points, playing tricks and defense, and not just a long string of spades.

11. ♠ A Q J 9 x x x x   Bid 4 ♠, as a preempt.
    ♡ x
    ◊ Q 10 x
    ♣ x

Let's review your options when your right-hand opponent opens the bidding with one of a suit:

PASS	without a good suit or with no prospects of finding a good suit. This may be the right action even if you have an opening bid or more in high cards.
OVERCALL	with a good suit, always five or more cards, and about an opening bid or slightly more.
JUMP OVERCALL	with a good six- or seven-card suit but a poor hand. This bid is used as a mild preempt.
PREEMPT	with a good seven-card or longer suit.
MAKE A TAKEOUT DOUBLE	with either (1) an opening bid or better plus support for all the unbid suits, or (2) a powerful hand, 18 points or more, and a good suit of your own.
OVERCALL 1 NT	with 16-18 high-card points and some high cards in the opponents' suit.
CUE-BID THE OPPONENTS' SUIT	with a hand that you would have opened with a forcing two-bid.

Now let's move to the other side of the table. Suppose your left-hand opponent opened 1 ♡, and your partner has doubled. This is a TAKEOUT DOUBLE. He wants you to bid so that your side can locate a playable trump suit. Let's look at some hands and see how you would respond.

1. ♠ Q x x x   This is not an uncommon nightmare.
    ♡ x x x   Your left-hand opponent, who opened,
    ◊ x x x   and your partner, who doubled for take-
    ♣ x x x   out, both have good hands, so you may
                  have nothing. Nevertheless, bid 1 ♠.
Your partner did not ask if you had any points — he asked you to pick a suit. As we will see, he must be prepared for the possibility that you have little or no strength.

161

2. ♠ x x   Bid 2 ◊. This will only hurt for a minute,
    ♡ x x x   we promise you. Partner either has good
    ◊ J x x x x   diamond support or he has an excellent
    ♣ x x x   hand with a suit of his own.

3. ♠ A Q 10 x   You must not bid only 1 ♠ here, for how
    ♡ x x   will partner know that you have 10 points
    ◊ J x x x   and not a completely worthless hand?
    ♣ K x x   Jump to 2 ♠. This bid shows about 10-12
                        points and invites partner to go on to game

but is not forcing. Partner can pass with a minimum takeout double.
Remember that his takeout double promises at least an opening bid
or more. When you hold a hand as good at this one, there may be
an easy game available.

4. ♠ J x x   Respond 3♣, inviting partner to bid
    ♡ A x   further if he has more than just a minimum
    ◊ x x x   takeout double.
    ♣ K Q 10 x x

5. ♠ K Q 10 x x   Bid 4♠, a contract that you expect to
    ♡ A x   make. Your opening bid plus partner's
    ◊ K x x   takeout double add up to a game. And
    ♣ x x x   spades is where you want to play it.

6. ♠ Q x x x x   Bid 1♠. Things could be a lot worse.
    ♡ x x
    ◊ J x x
    ♣ Q x x

7. ♠ x x   Respond 1 NT. This bid shows a fair
    ♡ K 10 x   hand. Do not bid 1 NT to show a bad
    ◊ A x x x   hand. If your hand contains no high card
    ♣ J x x x   strength, that is the time to look for a suit
                        so that you can make an extra trick or two

with your trumps. A 1 NT response to a takeout double shows 6-9
points (about the same as a 1 NT response to an opening bid), balanced
pattern and a high card in the opponents' suit.

8. ♠ J x
   ♥ A Q x
   ◊ K x x x
   ♣ J x x x

   Respond 2 NT. This is invitational to a game in notrump and shows 10-12 points, balanced pattern, and something good in the opponents' suit.

9. ♠ K x x x
   ♥ x x
   ◊ K J x x
   ♣ x x x

   Respond 1 ♠. With a choice of suits, bid the major suit.

10. ♠ A x
    ♥ Q J 10 9 x
    ◊ Q x x
    ♣ x x x

    Pass. On rare occasions, you may convert your partner's takeout double to a penalty double by passing. But you must have a fair hand and a SOLID HOLDING IN THE OPPONENTS' SUIT BEFORE YOU CAN FEEL CONFIDENT OF DEFEATING THE OPPONENTS' CONTRACT.

Let's review the options you have in RESPONDING TO PARTNER'S TAKEOUT DOUBLE:

RESPONDING TO A TAKEOUT DOUBLE	
WITH 0-9 points:	— bid a suit as cheaply as possible. — bid 1 NT with balanced pattern, 6-9 points and something good in the opponents' suit.
WITH 10-12 points:	— jump in your best suit, to invite game. — jump to 2 NT with balanced pattern and something good in the opponents' suit, to invite game in notrump.
WITH 13 points up	— jump to game in your best suit. — jump to 3 NT with balanced pattern and something good in the opponents' suit.

(There is actually a third option available to responder if he has a very strong hand — A CUEBID of the opponents' suit shows a desire to bid game but doubt as to which game contract is best.)

163

DO NOT PASS a takeout double unless you have a fair hand and a LONG, SOLID HOLDING IN THE OPPONENTS' SUIT.

Now let's get back to the takeout doubler's hand. Suppose that your right-hand opponent opened 1 ♥, you doubled for takeout, and your partner responded 1 ♠. What should you do with:

1. ♠ A Q x x
   ♥ x x
   ◇ A J x x
   ♣ K x x

You must remember that you forced partner to respond. He may have no points at all, and certainly has fewer than 10 since he failed to jump. Game is out of the question. In fact, partner may need everything you have to make his 1 ♠ contract. Pass. You need a lot more to bid higher when partner may be broke.

2. ♠ A Q x x
   ♥ x
   ◇ A K x x
   ♣ K 10 x x

This time you are justified in raising to 2 ♠. But do not bid more. Don't go wild with enthusiasm just because partner responded in a suit as you asked him to. He may have no points. There is some chance for game, however, since he could have as much as 8-9. Show him your extra strength.

3. ♠ A K Q x
   ♥ x
   ◇ A K x x
   ♣ A Q x x

Bid 4 ♠. Even if partner has a terrible hand, he should have a chance.

4. ♠ K Q x
   ♥ x x
   ◇ A x x
   ♣ A K Q x x

Bid just 2 ♣. If partner has no points, you will need everything you've got to make even eight tricks. Remember, a takeout double followed by a bid shows substantial extra strength. Partner will bid over your 2 ♣ if he has any points and thinks there might be a game. Otherwise, you are just as well off at an eight-trick contract.

AFTER MAKING A TAKEOUT DOUBLE, DO NOT BID AGAIN UNLESS YOU HAVE CONSIDERABLY MORE THAN A MINIMUM. PARTNER HAS BEEN FORCED TO RESPOND AND MAY HAVE A VERY POOR HAND.

TEST YOUR COMPREHENSION OF THE MATERIAL IN THIS CHAPTER:

QUIZ ON ACTING OVER THE OPPONENTS' OPENING BID:

I. Your right-hand opponent has opened the bidding with 1 ◊. What should you do with these hands?

1. ♠ Axx	2. ♠ xx	3. ♠ AQJxx
♡ Kxx	♡ Axx	♡ Axx
◊ Qxx	◊ KQ10x	◊ xx
♣ AJxx	♣ Axxx	♣ Jxx

4. ♠ xx	5. ♠ KQ10xxx	6. ♠ x
♡ Ax	♡ x	♡ KQJxxxx
◊ Qxxx	◊ xx	◊ xx
♣ KJxxx	♣ J10xx	♣ Jxx

7. ♠ Kxxx	8. ♠ AK	9. ♠ Ax
♡ Axx	♡ AQJxx	♡ Kxx
◊ xx	◊ xx	◊ AJx
♣ AQxx	♣ Axxx	♣ KQxxx

10. ♠ AKJxx
♡ AKQxx
◊ x
♣ Kx

QUIZ ON RESPONDING TO A TAKEOUT DOUBLE:

II. Your left-hand opponent has opened 1♣ and your partner doubled for takeout. What should you do with these hands:

1. ♠ Qxxx	2. ♠ Qxxx	3. ♠ AQxx
♡ xxx	♡ Qx	♡ xx
◊ xx	◊ xx	◊ AJx
♣ xxxx	♣ Jxxxx	♣ xxxx

4. ♠ Axxxx	5. ♠ xx	6. ♠ xx
♡ AK	♡ Kxx	♡ Axx
◊ Jxx	◊ Qxxx	◊ Kxxx
♣ xxx	♣ Kxxx	♣ KJxx

7.	♠ Jx	8.	♠ xx	9.	♠ xx
	♡ Jxx		♡ Axx		♡ Axx
	◊ KJxxxx		◊ Kxx		◊ KQJxx
	♣ AQ		♣ KJ1098		♣ xxx

10.	♠ Kxx
	♡ AKx
	◊ Axxxx
	♣ xx

QUIZ ON REBIDDING AFTER YOU HAVE MADE A TAKEOUT DOUBLE:

III.   Your right-hand opponent has opened 1 ♡, you doubled for takeout, and your partner responded 1 ♠. What should you do with:

1.	♠ AKJx	2.	♠ AQxx	3.	♠ AQxx
	♡ xx		♡ x		♡ x
	◊ Kxxx		◊ AKxx		◊ AKQx
	♣ Qxx		♣ Kxxx		♣ KQJx

4.	♠ AJx
	♡ xx
	◊ AKx
	♣ KQJxx

SOLUTIONS:

I.			II.			III.		
	1.	Pass		1.	1♠		1.	Pass
	2.	Pass		2.	1♠		2.	2♠
	3.	1♠		3.	2♠		3.	4♠
	4.	Pass		4.	4♠		4.	2♣
	5.	2♠		5.	1 NT			
	6.	3♡		6.	2 NT			
	7.	Double		7.	3 NT			
	8.	Double		8.	Pass			
	9.	1 NT		9.	2◊			
	10.	2◊		10.	2♣			

Chapter 10

THE CHALLENGE OF BRIDGE

Throughout this book, we have been learning things that a beginning bridge player must know. A sound knowledge of the fundamentals is essential if you hope to enjoy playing the game and have a chance to win consistently. We've spent much of our time learning rules. Nevertheless, there is a lot more to bridge than adherence to rules. When you sit down at the bridge table, you have a chance to display imagination, creativity and logical thought.

In this last chapter, we have something different in mind. We want to show you a few hands that illustrate some of the finer points of the game of bridge. You are not expected to be able to execute the techniques we will discuss at this point in your bridge-playing career — even a very experienced player might not be able to play all of these hands correctly. But we do want you to see that these techniques exist, and that they are an important part of the game. We hope that seeing these hands will inspire you to learn still more about bridge.

1. DRAWING INFERENCES

Back in the second chapter, we looked at this combination of cards in our discussion on trick-taking.

K J x

A 10 x

To make three tricks with this holding, we said that declarer should try to guess which opponent held the missing queen, and then take a finesse through him. This is a two-way guess, since the finesse can be taken in either of two directions, and in principle it is a 50-50 proposition.

An expert declarer will guess this situation correctly a lot more than 50% of the time. How is that possible? There will often be some clues available to point his way to the missing queen, clues from the bidding or the play of the hand up to the point where he makes his guess.

Let's put this card combination into the context of a hand:

♠ Q 10 x x
♡ K J x
◊ Q x x
♣ A J x

♠ A K x x x
♡ A 10 x
◊ x x
♣ Q 10 x

The bidding went:

East	South	West	North
Pass	1♠	Pass	3♠
Pass	4♠	(All Pass)	

The opening lead was the ◊ J which won the first trick. East won the second diamond with the king and tried to cash the ◊ A. You ruffed. Next, you drew two rounds of trumps with the ace and king. Both opponents followed; West had two little trumps, East had Jx. Now you tried the club finesse. It lost to East's king, and he returned a club. You won and now you must figure out the heart suit.

This is the same combination of cards we have above, with a two-way guess. This may have been a complete guess when the play began, but now that you have seen several tricks, it is no longer a guess. There are clues available, and in fact, a good declarer would know for sure where the ♡ Q was hiding! Does that sound like magic? It's just a little logic plus a little concentration.

East dealt and passed, and you and partner took over and bid to 4♠. During the play so far, you have seen East play the ◊ AK, the ♠ J, and the ♣ K. **How many high-card points is that?** *Eleven* high-card points. Now suppose that East had the ♡ Q. **How would the bidding have gone?** East would have opened the bidding, with his *thirteen* high-card points! So *West* must have the queen you are seeking.

That's not really so hard, is it? All we did was count to 13, and anybody can do that! This type of *logical reasoning* is an important part of bridge; in fact, this is what bridge is all about.

2. DECEPTION

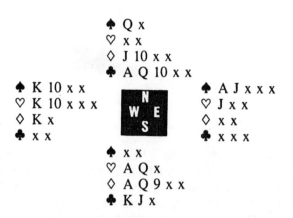

```
              ♠ Q x
              ♡ x x
              ◊ J 10 x x
              ♣ A Q 10 x x
♠ K 10 x x                      ♠ A J x x x
♡ K 10 x x x                    ♡ J x x
◊ K x                           ◊ x x
♣ x x                           ♣ x x x
              ♠ x x
              ♡ A Q x
              ◊ A Q 9 x x
              ♣ K J x
```

South chose to open 1 NT and North raised to 3 NT. West naturally led a low heart from his longest suit. East played his jack, and declarer won the trick with his ACE(!) He crossed to dummy with a club, and took the diamond finesse, which lost to the king. West naturally thought he had struck gold with his opening heart lead, and placing his partner with the ♡ Q, he led another low heart, expecting to run the entire heart suit. But declarer produced the ♡ Q and cashed the rest of his club and diamond winners, making 5 NT.

Now, **why do you suppose declarer won the first heart trick with the ace when he could have won more cheaply with his queen?** What would probably have happened if declarer had won the first trick with the ♡ Q? Put yourself into West's seat when he won the ◊ K. Knowing that declarer had a second heart stopper (with the ace), and knowing that a great many tricks in clubs and diamonds were clearly available to declarer, would you not switch to spades and the only chance to defeat 3 NT?

Declarer wanted to avoid a spade switch if the diamond finesse lost to West. His play of the ♡ A was designed to throw up a smokescreen by making the defenders think that their opening lead had been productive, when in fact he feared another suit, spades, a lot more. An imaginative play by declarer.

169

3. ENDPLAY

How would you play this hand as declarer in 3 NT?

♠ x x x
♡ A Q x x
◇ K x x
♣ x x x

♠ A Q
♡ K x x
◇ A J x x
♣ A Q x x

The opening lead is the ♣2. This is helpful, isn't it? If you had to lead clubs yourself, you would try a finesse by leading a low card from dummy to your queen. This might or might not win the trick. But if a club is led from your left, and you *get to play last* to the trick, your queen is bound to be a winner no matter which opponent has the king. The opening club lead offers you what is called a "free" finesse. East plays the ♣J at the first trick, and your queen scores.

Suppose you play the ♡K, ♡Q, and ♡A next. You hope for a 3-3 split that will make dummy's fourth heart a trick, but West discards a spade on the third round of hearts. At this point, you can finesse in either spades or diamonds for your ninth trick. **Which finesse should you prefer?**

This is really a tricky question, because the answer is, *neither* finesse should be taken. Instead, you should try to get the opponents to help you by giving you *another* free finesse. Suppose you play a club to your ace, and then give up the lead with a club. West will win this trick and will be able to cash one more club (his opening lead of the ♣2 suggests that he had a *four*-card suit to begin with), but what will he do then? He will have nothing left in his hand except spades and diamonds (we saw him show out on the third round of hearts, remember), so he will have to lead one of those suits. **Do you see what will happen?** Regardless of *which* suit he leads, you will get another free finesse, and you will be bound to make your ninth trick!

As a rule, it is best to get to play *last* to a trick. You can see what everybody else has played before you choose the most appropriate card to contribute. In fact, it can be good strategy for you to *give the opponents the lead* at a crucial moment in the play, so that they have to lead around to you, allowing you to play last. You might be able to make a trick in this way, by getting the opponents to help you, that you could *not* have made on your own. This technique, which is called an *endplay* or *throw-in,* is the one declarer used on this hand to make 3 NT. Good declarers routinely make extra tricks this way.

4. SQUEEZE

Suppose you have arrived in a 7 NT contract with these cards:

♠ A x x x x x
♡ A
◊ K J
♣ A Q J x

♠ K x
♡ Q x x x
◊ A Q 10 9 x
♣ K x

The opening lead is the ♣ 10. You can count 12 top tricks but there seems to be no way to develop the 13th trick you need without conceding the setting trick. **Is this a hopeless contract then?**

Let's look at all four hands and see if we can see a chance for declarer.

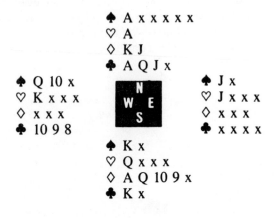

```
                    ♠ A x x x x x
                    ♡ A
                    ◊ K J
                    ♣ A Q J x
  ♠ Q 10 x           N            ♠ J x
  ♡ K x x x       W     E         ♡ J x x x
  ◊ x x x            S            ◊ x x x
  ♣ 10 9 8                        ♣ x x x x
                    ♠ K x
                    ♡ Q x x x
                    ◊ A Q 10 9 x
                    ♣ K x
```

Let's suppose declarer (with nothing better to do) starts cashing all his tricks, the clubs first, then the ♡A, then the diamonds. After you lead to trick ten, this will be the situation: (West still to play to trick ten.)

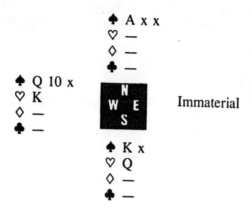

```
              ♠ A x x
              ♡ —
              ◊ —
              ♣ —
  ♠ Q 10 x
  ♡ K                 N
  ◊ —            W    E     Immaterial
  ♣ —                 S
              ♠ K x
              ♡ Q
              ◊ —
              ♣ —
```

What does poor West do? If he discards his ♡K, declarer makes the 13th trick with the ♡Q. If West throws a spade, dummy's last spade becomes a trick. West is *squeezed,* and the contract is bound to succeed.

A *squeeze* is another technique a good declarer can put to use to produce an extra trick as if by magic. A squeeze occurs when one of your opponents has something good in two (or more) suits and is unable to keep both of his holdings because he must make too many discards. There are several conditions that must be present before a squeeze will function and the possibilities for a squeeze are sometimes hard to see, even for an experienced player. But the successful execution of a squeeze is one of the biggest thrills you will have at the bridge table, This should be a goal of every aspiring bridge player.

QUIZ ON THE CHALLENGE OF BRIDGE:

1.
       ♠ x x x
       ♡ J 9 x
       ◊ K Q J x
       ♣ A x x

       ♠ A Q 10
       ♡ A 10 x
       ◊ A x x x
       ♣ Q x x

Contract: 3 NT
West leads a low spade, East plays the jack, and you win the queen.
How do you play to make your contract for certain?

2.
       ♠ x x
       ♡ x x x
       ◊ Q J x x
       ♣ A K x x

       ♠ A K J
       ♡ Q x
       ◊ A 10 x x x
       ♣ Q x x

Contract: 3 NT
West leads a low spade and East plays the ten. What is your best
chance to make this contract?

3.
                ♠ A x x
                ♡ A J x x
                ◊ x x x
                ♣ A K 10

                ♠ K Q 10 x x x
                ♡ Q x
                ◊ x x x
                ♣ x x

You reach a 4 ♠ contract after East opens the bidding with 1 NT (16-18 HCP). West leads the ◊ J. East cashes the ace, king, and queen, and shifts to a trump. How should you play?

4.
                ♠ A x x x
                ♡ J 10 x x
                ◊ K x x
                ♣ x x

                ♠ J x
                ♡ A Q 9 x x
                ◊ A Q x
                ♣ K J x

Contract: 4 ♡

You opened 1 ♡ *after three passes* and got to game in hearts. West leads the ♠K. You win the ace and take a heart finesse, losing to West's king. West cashes the ♠Q, and you ruff the next spade and draw trumps. Now should you lead a club to your king or a club to your jack?

5.   ♠ K x
                  ♡ J x x
                  ◇ J x x
                  ♣ K J x x x

                  ♠ x x
                  ♡ K Q 10 x x x
                  ◇ A
                  ♣ A 10 x x

Contract: 4 ♡

East opened the bidding 1 ♠. West leads a spade, and East wins the queen and ace. He cashes the ace of trumps and gets out with a trump, West following. With the trumps in, you play a club to the king, both opponents playing low, and a club back, East playing the nine. Do you play your ace or finesse your ten?

SOLUTIONS:

1. Cash enough diamond tricks to exhaust the opponents of that suit. Then lead a heart from dummy and play the ten from your hand (unless East plays an honor). If West wins the heart trick, he will be ENDPLAYED, forced to give you an extra trick no matter what suit he returns. Try out the various possibilities and see for yourself.

2. Win the first trick with the *king*. Then lead a club to dummy and try the diamond finesse. If it loses, you hope that West will lead spades again instead of shifting to a heart. If you win the first spade with the jack, West will know there is no future for his side of spades.

3. Cash the ♡ A and *run off all your trumps*. East, who must hold all the missing high cards for his 1 NT opening, will be SQUEEZED in hearts and clubs. He won't be able to hold his ♡ K and his club stopper. Try it and see for yourself.

4. Lead a club to your *king*. West would probably have opened the bidding with the ♠ KQ, the ♡ K, *and* the ♣ A. So the ♣ A should be on your right.

5. Play the ♣ A. If you finesse the ♣ 10, you are playing East for ♣ Q9x and West for a singleton. But West would probably had *led* a singleton club against this contract if he had one. That would be a very attractive line of defense to anyone. So the clubs are very likely divided 2-2, and the queen will fall under your ace.

"ABOVE THE LINE":	Scoring of points won for overtricks, penalties and bonuses.
ACTIVE DEFENSE:	The defenders' approach when they are desperate for tricks because declarer threatens to get discards for his losers.
ASSUMPTION:	Technique by which declarer or defender bases his play on the premise that the contract can be made or set.
ATTITUDE:	Defensive signal that shows like or dislike for a suit.
AVOIDANCE:	Technique in play whereby a dangerous opponent is kept from gaining the lead.
AUCTION:	See BIDDING.
BALANCED HAND:	Hand containing no void suit or singleton, and no more than one doubleton.
BALANCING:	Backing into the auction after the opponents have stopped low, counting on partner to hold some values.

"BELOW THE LINE":	Scoring of points that count toward making a game.
BID:	Call in the auction that promises to take a certain number of tricks in the play and suggests a suit as trumps (or suggests the play be at notrump).
BIDDING:	The first phase of each hand of bridge, when the players on both sides have a chance to bid for the right to name the trump suit and suggest how many tricks they expect their side to win in the play.
BLACKWOOD:	A conventional bid of 4 NT that asks partner to reveal, through an artificial response, the number of aces he holds.
BOOK:	(1) The first six tricks won by declarer's side; (2) the number of tricks the defenders must win before they begin to score undertricks.
BROKEN SEQUENCE:	Sequence such as QJ9, which contains a gap between the middle and lowest of the three cards.
BROKEN SUIT:	Suit which contains no cards adjacent in rank.
BUSINESS DOUBLE:	Penalty double.
CALL:	Any action, including a pass, taken in the bidding.
CAPTAINCY:	The bidding principle whereby one partner is obliged to take responsibility for placing the contract once his partner's hand is limited in strength.
CARD SENSE:	An intangible quality that those skilled in card play seem to possess.
CHICAGO SCORING:	A type of scoring in which every deal is taken as a separate entity. There are no rubbers or partscores carried over the next deal.
COME-ON:	An encouraging attitude signal.
COMPETITIVE BIDDING:	Auctions in which both sides bid.
CONSTRUCTIVE BIDDING:	Auctions in which one side tries to reach its best contract without interference.
CONTRACT:	The number of tricks that the side that wins the auction undertakes to make.
CONTROL:	Holding that prevents the opponents from taking two fast tricks in that suit. An ace; king; or singleton or void, if some other suit is trumps.
CONVENTION:	A bid to which an artificial meaning has been assigned.
CROSS-RUFF:	A play technique in which cards are trumped in both partnership hands alternately, on several successive tricks.

CUEBID:	(1) A bid of an opponent's suit, intended to show great strength.
	(2) A bid of a suit in which a control is held, intended to facilitate slam investigation.
	(3) Any of several conventional cuebids, such as Michaels.
CUT:	The division of the pack into rough halves prior to the deal.
DEAL:	The distribution of the 52 cards, 13 to each player face down, that begins each hand of bridge.
DECLARER:	The player who tries to make the contract by using both his own and dummy's cards.
DEFENDERS:	The partnership that opposes declarer and tries to defeat the contract.
DISCARD:	A played card which is not of the suit led nor of the trump suit.
DOUBLE:	A call generally intended to increase the penalty suffered by the opponents if their last bid becomes an unsuccessful çontract.
DOUBLE FINESSE:	A combination of plays in which declarer finesses against two missing honors.
DOUBLE SQUEEZE:	An advanced type of squeeze in which each defender is squeezed in turn.
DOUBLETON:	A holding of two cards in a suit.
DRAW TRUMPS:	Technique in which declarer leads trumps, forcing the opponents to follow suit, until their trumps are exhausted.
DROP:	Cause a missing high card to fall by playing a still higher card or cards.
DUMMY:	Declarer's partner. The term is also applied to the dummy's cards, placed face up on the table.
DUMMY REVERSAL:	Technique by which declarer makes extra tricks by ruffing several times in his own hand and ultimately drawing trumps with dummy's trump holding.
DUPLICATE BRIDGE:	A contest in which the same hands are played several times by different players, allowing for a comparison of results.
DUPLICATION OF VALUES:	The condition in which the high cards and distribution of the partnership hands are ill-suited to each other.
ECHO:	A high-low sequence of play used to signal attitude or count.
ENDPLAY:	Technique by which a trick is gained through deliberately giving an opponent the lead in a position where he has no safe exit.
ENTRY:	A card used as a means of gaining the lead.
EQUALS:	Cards that are adjacent in rank, or that become adjacent when the cards that separate them are played.

FALSE CARD:	A card played with intent to deceive.
FALSE PREFERENCE:	A preference offered without true support, typically with two cards.
FINESSE:	Maneuver by which it is hoped to win a trick with an intermediate card, by playing that card after one opponent has already played.
FIT:	A holding which suggests that suit will adequately serve as trumps.
FIVE-CARD MAJORS:	A bidding style in which an opening bid of 1 ♠ or 1 ♡ promises five or more cards.
FOLLOWING SUIT:	Each player's first obligation in the play, to play a card of the same suit that was led to the trick if possible.
FORCING BID:	A bid that compels partner to take further action.
FORCING DEFENSE:	The defenders' approach when they try to exhaust declarer of trumps by repeatedly forcing him to ruff.
FORCING PASS:	Pass made over an opponent's bid, which compels partner to double the opponents or bid further.
FREE BID:	Bid made when the alternative would be to pass and allow partner the next opportunity to act. Typically based on sound values.
FREE RAISE:	Raise of partner's suit in competition. Not a significant term, since such a raise does *not* imply extra strength.
GAME:	(1) A unit of scoring, two of which comprise a rubber; a game is won by the first partnership to score 100 or more points below the line.
	(2) Any contract which will allow the partnership to score game if fulfilled.
GAME TRY:	A bid that suggests interest in game and asks partner to assess his values and make the final decision.
GERBER:	A conventional bid of 4 ♣ that asks partner to reveal, through an artificial response, the number of aces he holds.
GRAND SLAM FORCE:	A bid of 5 NT, when used to show interest in bidding a grand slam in the agreed trump suit provided partner holds certain honors in trumps.
HIGH-CARD POINT COUNT:	Method of hand evaluation in which a numerical value is assigned to each high honor.
HONOR:	Ace, king, queen, jack or ten.
HONORS:	Bonus available in the scoring for a holding of four or all five honors in the trump suit in the same hand; or, at notrump, all four aces in the same hand.
HOLD-UP:	Refusal to take a winner, often for purposes of disrupting the opponents' communication.
INFERENCE:	A conclusion logically deduced from evidence.

179

INFERENTIAL COUNT:	An assessment of the entire distribution of the concealed hands, based on evidence from the bidding and the early play.
INTERIOR SEQUENCE:	Holding such as KJ109x, in which the equals are accompanied by some higher card.
INTERMEDIATES:	Cards which may become winners as the cards that outrank them are played.
INVITATIONAL BID:	Bid that asks partner to continue to game or slam with maximum values.
JORDAN:	The conventional understanding in which a jump to 2 NT by responder, after the opener's bid is doubled for takeout, shows a limit raise in opener's suit.
JUMP OVERCALL:	A suit bid made usually (as the next bid) after an opponent has opened the bidding, but at a higher level than necessary.
JUMP SHIFT:	(1) A jump of one level in a new suit by opening bidder. (2) A jump of one level in a new suit by responder. Either action implies great strength.
LEG:	A fulfilled partscore, a step toward game.
LEAD:	The first card played to a trick.
LIMIT BID:	Bid that promises no more than a pre-agreed amount of high-card strength.
LIMIT RAISE:	Direct double raise of partner's opening one-bid that promises invitational values only.
LONG CARDS:	Low cards that become winners because they are the only cards of their suit which remain in play.
MAJOR SUITS:	Spades and hearts.
MATCHPOINT SCORING:	Type of scoring used in duplicate (tournament) bridge, in which several different results from an identical deal are compared.
MAXIMUM:	Holding the greatest possible values for one's previous bidding.
MINIMUM:	Holding the fewest possible values for one's previous bidding.
NEGATIVE RESPONSE:	Bid, often artificial, that denies good values; made in response to partner's forcing action.
NOTRUMP:	Strain in which the play is conducted with no trump suit. The highest card played of the suit that is led to a trick wins that trick.
OBLIGATORY FALSECARD:	Falsecard that will lead to a certain loss if not played.
OBLIGATORY FINESSE:	The handling of certain suit combinations in which declarer plays a low card from both hands, hoping his opponent will be forced to follow suit with a high honor.
OFFSIDE:	Unfavorably placed for a finesse to work.

ONSIDE:	Favorably placed for a finesse to work.
OPEN THE BIDDING:	To make the first bid in the auction.
OPENING LEAD:	The lead to the first trick, made by the defender to declarer's left.
OVERCALL:	Bid in a suit after the opponents have opened the bidding (but before partner has taken any action).
OVERTRICKS:	Tricks taken in excess of those bid.
PARTIAL:	A partscore.
PARTNERSHIP:	Two players working as a unit. Bridge is played by two competing partnerships. Partners sit opposite each other. Trust and cooperation between partners are important features of the game.
PARTSCORE:	A contract below the level of game. Successful partscores can accumulate toward scoring game.
PASS:	Call in the auction when the player does not wish to bid, double or redouble.
PASSED OUT:	Deal on which none of the four players bid. Calls for another deal.
PASSIVE DEFENSE:	Defenders' approach when dummy is short of winners and the defense can wait on its tricks.
PENALTY DOUBLE:	Double made for a larger penalty, in the expectation that the contract will fail.
PERCENTAGE PLAY:	Line of play which will succeed most often, determined on only a mathematical basis.
PLAIN SUIT:	Any suit other than trumps.
POINT COUNT:	The method of hand evaluation whereby a numerical value is assigned to the possible trick-taking features of a hand.
POSITIVE RESPONSE:	Response to partner's forcing opening that promises certain good values.
PREEMPTIVE BID:	Bid made not for constructive purposes but merely to crowd the opponents and make it hard for them to bid accurately.
PREFERENCE:	A bid which chooses between two possible strains partner has offered.
PREPARED BID:	An opening bid in a low-ranking suit (often, a suit of only three cards), made so that a higher-ranking suit will provide an easy, space-saving rebid.
PRIMARY VALUES:	Aces and kings.
PROPRIETIES:	That section of the Laws of Contract Bridge that deals with ethics and etiquette.

PSYCHIC BID:	A bluff bid, made on a non-existent suit or without values, intended to intimidate the opposition.
QUANTITATIVE SLAM (GAME) TRY:	Bid that asks partner to pass or bid on, based strictly on the number of high-card values he holds.
RAISE:	A bid in the same suit (or notrump) that partner has just bid, often confirming that suit as trumps.
REBID:	(1) Bid the same suit a second time. (2) Any bid chosen at one's second turn.
REDOUBLE:	Call available in the auction which doubles, in turn, points scored if the contract is played doubled.
RESPONDER:	Opening bidder's partner.
RESTRICTED CHOICE:	A mathematical concept, based on the opponents' possible play from a holding of several equal cards, that may be helpful in determining the play of certain suit combinations.
REVERSE:	(1) A rebid in a new suit, such that the level of the contract will be increased if partner shows a preference for the first suit. (2) To bid in such a way, thereby showing a strong hand.
REVOKE:	Failure to follow suit when holding a card of the suit led.
RUBBER:	Unit of scoring in bridge, won by the side to first make two games, and carrying a large bonus.
RUFF:	To trump.
RUFF-AND-DISCARD (RUFF-SLUFF):	The lead of a suit in which both declarer and dummy are void, allowing declarer to discard a loser from the hand of his choice while he ruffs in the other.
RULE OF 11:	Device, applicable if the lead is known to be fourth-highest, that may be used to make judgments in the play. Subtract the rank of the spot led from 11. The remainder shows the number of higher cards held by the hands, other than leader's.
SACRIFICE:	A deliberate overbid, but one in which declarer expects to be penalized fewer points than the opponents would score if allowed to play their own contract.
SAFETY PLAY:	The handling of a combination of cards so as to insure against a devastating loss of tricks.
SECOND-HAND:	(1) The next player to have a chance to bid after the dealer. (2) The player who plays immediately after a trick is led to.
SECONDARY VALUES:	Queens and jacks.
SEMI-BALANCED HAND:	Hand which is neither balanced nor unbalanced by definition, 2-2-4-5 or 2-2-3-6 pattern.
SEQUENCE:	Three or more cards adjacent in rank, the highest one of which is an honor.

SET:	To defeat the contract.
SHORT CLUB:	See PREPARED BID.
SHUT-OUT BID:	A preemptive bid.
SIGNAL:	Any of several conventional understandings through which the defenders can give each other information by means of the card they play.
SIGNOFF:	Bid that suggests that partner pass.
SIMPLE SQUEEZE:	Type of squeeze in which a single opponent is squeezed.
SINGLETON:	A holding of only one card in a suit.
SLAM:	A contract for 12 or 13 tricks, carrying a bonus in the scoring.
SPOT CARD:	Card below the rank of an honor.
SQUEEZE:	Technique, most often used by declarer, in which a defender is forced to relinquish a winner no matter what card he chooses.
STANDARD AMERICAN:	The bidding system most commonly used in America; essentially, the Goren style, with gadgets and refinements added.
STOPPER:	A card or combination of cards certain to produce a trick in a suit.
STRIP:	Play a suit or suits so as to make it impossible for an opponent to lead that suit or lead it safely.
SUIT-PREFERENCE SIGNAL:	Defensive signal which bears no relation to its own suit but shows interest in another, specific suit.
SURROUNDING PLAY:	Maneuver in which a defender breaks a suit by leading a high card that is part of a near-sequential holding.
SYSTEM:	The total framework in which the partnership assigns well-defined meanings to its bids and bidding sequences.
TABLE PRESENCE:	The ability to draw inferences from the extraneous things that happen at the table.
TAKEOUT DOUBLE:	Double that requests partner not to pass but to choose a suit (or notrump) to play in.
TEMPORIZE:	Bid a suit (often, an unplayable suit), in the expectation of supporting partner's suit later. May be required if no immediate raise is appropriate.
TENACE:	An honor or combination of honors which will be most valuable if the holder is fourth-hand to play; e.g., AQ, KJ.
THIRD HAND:	In the auction, dealer's partner. In the play, leader's partner.
THIRD-SEAT OPENING:	An opening bid after two passes that may be based on sub-minimum values. Often it is intended as mainly lead-directing and mildly preemptive.

THROW-IN:	See ENDPLAY.
TRAP PASS:	Pass made with substantial values, including strength in the opponent's suit, in the hope of making a successful penalty double later.
TREATMENT:	A particular way of assigning a natural meaning to a bid or sequence of bids.
TRICK:	Four cards played in sequence, one by each player at the table, going clockwise.
TRUMPS:	The suit determined in the bidding to be that of the contract.
TRUMP CONTROL:	Technique by which declarer makes possession of the trump suit work to his advantage, exhausting the opponents of their trumps so he can safely establish and cash other winners.
TRUMP COUP:	The advanced play by which declarer can avoid losing a trick to an outstanding trump honor by forcing the defender to ruff and be overruffed.
TRUMP ECHO:	The high-low sequence of play in the trump suit, used in defense to show an odd number of trumps.
TRUMP PROMOTION:	Defensive technique in which declarer is forced to either ruff low and be overruffed or ruff high at the later cost of a trick.
TRUMP SUPPORT:	Usually four or more cards in partner's suit. Under some circumstances, three or fewer cards.
UNBALANCED HAND:	Hand containing a void suit or singleton.
UNBLOCK:	Play by declarer or defenders so as to allow the uninterrupted run of a long suit by proper management of the smaller cards.
UNDERTRICKS:	Tricks which declarer has bid but fails to take.
UPPERCUT:	Defensive technique in which a defender ruffs in with a trump intermediate and declarer is obliged to weaken his trump holding by overruffing.
VOID:	A suit in which no cards are held.
VULNERABILITY:	Condition in the scoring, achieved when one game has been won toward completion of the rubber.
WEAK TWO-BID:	Modern treatment in which an opening bid of 2♠, 2♡ or 2◇ shows a good six-card suit and about an average hand in high cards.

What the Proprieties Are About:

In a game such as poker, all sorts of at-the-table gamesmanship is allowed. In bridge, *skill in choosing a bid or play is emphasized.* A strict code of ethics and courtesy is part of the game. The better the players in the game, the higher the standard of ethics is likely to be. A higher standard of ethics is demanded in tournament play than in a social game at home. The purpose of the *Proprieties,* that section of the Laws of bridge that deals with conduct and ethics, is to make the game more enjoyable for everyone, no matter what the situation.

Please take time to read these excerpts from the Proprieties, as taken from the Laws of Duplicate Contract Bridge. If you observe the principles set down here, you will find yourself respected as both a partner and an opponent.

Conduct and Etiquette:

A player should maintain at all times a courteous attitude toward his partner and the opponents. He should carefully avoid any remark or action that might cause annoyance or embarrassment to another player, or that might interfere with another player's enjoyment of the game.

As a matter of courtesy, a play should refrain from:

Paying insufficient attention;

Making gratuitous comments during the play as to the auction or the adequacy of the contract;

Detaching a card from his hand before it is his turn to
play;

Arranging the cards he has played to previous tricks in a
disorderly manner or mixing his cards together before
the result of the deal has been agreed to;

Making a questionable claim or concession; or

Prolonging the play unnecessarily.

It is a breach of the Proprieties to:

Use different designations for the same call ("A Club,"
"I'll bid a club," etc., are incorrect. "One club" is the
only proper form).

Indicate any approval or disapproval of a call or play.

185

Indicate the expectation or intention of winning or losing a trick before play to that trick has been completed.

Comment or act during the auction or play to call attention to a significant incident thereof, or to the state of the score, or to the number of tricks that will be required for success.

Look intently at any other player during the auction or play, or at another player's hand for the purpose of seeing his cards or observing the place from which he draws a card.

Vary the normal tempo of bidding or play for the purpose of disconcerting the other players.

Communication Between Partners:

Communication between partners during the auction and play should be effected only by means of the calls and plays themselves. Calls should be made in a uniform tone without special emphasis or inflection, and without undue haste or hesitation. Plays should be made without emphasis, gesture or mannerism, and so far as possible, at a uniform rate.

It is improper for communication between partners to be effected through the *manner* in which calls and plays are made, through extraneous remarks or gestures, or through questions asked of the opponents or explanations given to them. When a player has available to him improper information from his partner's remark, question, explanation, gesture, mannerism, special emphasis, inflection, haste or hesitation, *he should carefully avoid taking any advantage that might accrue to his side.*

If it is determined that a player chose from among logical alternative actions one that could reasonably have been suggested by his partner's tempo, manner or remark, and this results in damage to innocent opponents, the score on the deal should be adjusted in favor of the innocent side. (Such an outcome *by no means implies* that the side that committed an infraction did so *deliberately*. The very problem with, say, hesitations, is that it is almost impossible for a player's objectivity not to be clouded by the fact that his partner has huddled. Who can say that he will not be *subconsciously* influenced by the huddle? Therefore, it is common practice today to routinely give redress to the innocent side in such situations.)

It is improper to have special understandings with partner regarding your bids and play of which the opponents are unaware. The opponents are entitled to know about that fancy new bidding Convention you and partner had decided to try out, and you are obliged to announce it to them before the game starts.

The Laws prescribe no formal penalty for violating any of the *Proprieties*. However, players who are careless and get to be known for a low standard of ethics will find that fewer and fewer players are willing to play with them.

A Note on Partnership Rapport:

There are many bridge players who look on partner as a necessary evil, but your success at the bridge table will depend in great part

on how well your partner performs. *Everything* that happens within your partnership can affect what kind of results you get, so your partner's morale should be important to you.

Nobody likes harsh criticism under any circumstances, but for people who play bridge seriously, the game is a real ego trip. We are sensitive about our game and our mistakes. If you point out your partner's errors right at the table (or, worse, if you are downright abusive), you are unlikely to accomplish anything constructive. On the contrary, you will probably get partner to dwell on his errors and induce him to play even worse.

A partnership at bridge is two people trying to act as one in an emotionally-charged setting. Recognize that when one player criticizes his partner, it is because he views partner's error as a direct reflection on his own ability; his sensitivity has been ruffled.

You should always assume that your partner wants to win as badly as you do, and he is trying as hard as he can. Therefore, withhold any criticism until after the game. Instead, you should be interested in *building* up his ego. If he makes an error, tell him that you would probably have done the same thing under the circumstances; or that he probably had what he thought was a good reason at the time he made his misguided bid or play. Give his ego a chance to recover and he will play harder for the rest of the game.

Do your partner, your partnership and yourself a favor. Apply the Golden Rule when your partner makes an error.

— NOTES —

Brewster Library
Brewster, Mass.